DATE DUE

NOV 1 5 1996	
MAR 3 1 1997	
MAY 2 2 1997	
OCT 2 8 1998	
APR 2 9 2014	

BRODART, CO.   Cat. No. 23-221-003

Intimate Relations

INTIMATE RELATIONS

The Natural History of Desire

Liam Hudson & Bernadine Jacot

Yale University Press
New Haven & London   1995

Set in Linotronic Galliard by SX Composing Ltd, Essex
Printed and bound in Great Britain by Biddles Ltd,
Guildford and Kings Lynn

Library of Congress Cataloging-in-Publication Data

Hudson, Liam.
    Intimate relations: the natural history of desire / Liam Hudson
and Bernadine Jacot.
        p.   cm.
    Includes bibliographical references and index.
    ISBN 0–300–06293–1
    1. Intimacy (Psychology)   2. Sex differences (Psychology)
3. Women — Psychology.   4. Men — Psychology.   I. Jacot, Bernadine.
II. Title.
BF575.I5H83   1995
158'.2 — dc20   95–7788
                                                                          CIP

A catalogue record for this book is available from the British Library.

Arricchiamoci delle nostre reciproche differenze.
We are enriched by our reciprocate differences.
Enrichissons-nous de nos différences mutuelles.
Enriquezcámonos de nuestras mutuas diferencias.

Paul Valéry

Ogni oggetto amato è il centro di un paradiso.
Every loved thing is the centre of a paradise.
L'objet de notre amour est le centre d'un paradis.
Todo objeto querido es el centro de un paraíso.

Novalis
(Chocolate box mottoes, Baci, Perugina, 1992)

Contents

Acknowledgements

ALTHOUGH RELATIVELY SHORT, THE present text has taken nearly four years to write; and in that time it has undergone more major changes than we care to recall. While many friends and colleagues have contributed to this process, and several have read and commented upon individual chapters, none has seen the text as a whole in anything approaching its published form. So rather than naming these friends and colleagues, and implicitly coopting them to arguments which they may consider mistaken, we have thanked them in private. Should they see this text and have the patience to read it, we hope they will appreciate how radical are the improvements their help has wrought.

London   L.H.
March 1995   B.J.

Introduction

IN 1991, WE PUBLISHED a book – *The Way Men Think* – which had at its centre the idea of the 'male wound'. In order to establish themselves as male, we argued, small boys must separate themselves from their mothers, and it is this separation which gives rise to many of the mental characteristics subsequently recognised in adulthood as typically 'male'.[1]

Beckoning as we wrote was a further argument about the way women think; and, beyond that, a third about men and women together and about the incompatibilities on which their intimacies with one another seem so often to founder. One book has a way of writing itself in the margins of another; and in drafting *The Way Men Think* we were, to a greater extent than we realised, sketching into place the rudiments of *Intimate Relations*: the subtle but systematic nature of the differences between the minds of men and women, and of their attitudes towards each other.

Our interest now lies in clarifying the nature of close relationships between people who are – and see themselves to be – dissimilar, and doing so in the light of detailed evidence about the lives people actually lead. As our argument unfolds, we return, time and again, to the same analogy: that between intimacy and art. Like works of art, intimacies are primarily exercises of the imagination. Both depend on the fashioning of something precious from the mundane.

Our argument, then, has two themes:

That psychological differences between the sexes are both deeply engrained and imaginatively galvanising; and

That there exists a parallel between art and intimate relations.

The first three chapters outline our theory of early childhood development and its implications for the lives of adults. A 'thought experiment' is used to show that psychological differences between adult men and women are intuitively grasped, but difficult, often, to put into words. Chapters 4, 5 and 6 outline the current state of play: a disillusionment about close relations between the sexes which is exacerbated, we believe, by both misrepresentations of fact and mistaken assumptions. In our three remaining chapters, we offer a more optimistic view. Chapter 7 describes the translation of turbulent emotion into manageable form; and Chapter 8 considers the tensions and ambiguities of art and intimacy side by side. Having started with a thought experiment, we end with a conjecture: in Chapter 9, we argue that certain values may arise spontaneously from erotic intimacy, and in that sense be natural to it.

Before we begin, we have a definition to offer. We give this, not in the hope of pinning an elusive noun permanently into place, but as a first approximation. 'Intimacy' is a word with a longish history. The OED gives usages that go back to the seventeenth and early eighteenth centuries. The first is 'the quality or condition of being intimate'; the second and third those of 'close familiarity', and, euphemistically, of 'illicit sexual intercourse'. 'Intimate' in turn is given several meanings which slide across one another like the circles of a Venn diagram:

Inmost, most inward, deep-seated; hence, Essential, intrinsic (1632);

Pertaining to the inmost thoughts and feelings (1671);

Close in acquaintance or association; characterized by familiarity; very familiar (no date);

Closeness of observation, knowledge, or the like (1714);

Intimate connexion or union (1720).

Buried in this semantic cluster is the sense of a reciprocal traffic in thoughts and needs that springs up between those who know one another well and remain erotically alive to one another. It is in the midst of this traffic that the imagination thrives.

While our argument is rooted in heterosexuality – the mutual fascination of individuals who are categorically dissimilar – this preoccupation is by no means exclusive. The explanations we offer embrace all those who are fascinated by the detection of similarity in difference and difference in similarity; and they do so irrespective of whether the similarities and differences in question are clear-cut or elusive, or of whether or not they have a foundation in the way the body works or looks.

It is sometimes said that two great frontiers remain for science: the exploration of outer space and the discovery of the principles governing the central nervous system. This book is written for those alert to the existence of a third; intellectually, fully as demanding as the other two – not least because, here, knowledge so obviously interacts with what it seeks to describe and explain. *It concerns what happens when dissimilar systems of need and imaginative representation meet and merge.*

CHAPTER ONE

Allowing the Clockwork to Run

IN THIS CHAPTER, WE outline our view of psychological development, pointing to processes that impart a bias of one kind to the workings of the male imagination and a bias of another to those of the female imagination.

The Role of the Imagination

The theory of development adopted in *The Way Men Think* has been quite widely used by psychologists, psychiatrists and psycho-analysts, and its form is simple.[1] It focuses on children's needs to:

Establish a sense of themselves as male or female (their *gender identity*); and

Find a stable focus for their desires (their *object choice*).

These undertakings are fuelled by:

The instinctual needs for *attachment* and *separation*, and their attendant fears of being engulfed or abandoned.

And in the case of small boys, they give rise to two more specific developmental processes:

The severing of the child's symbiotic bond with his mother (*dis-identification*); and,

His subsequent alignment with the father (*counter-identification*).[2]

What distinguishes our use of this theoretical model from previous formulations is that we treat the imagination as the mind's central function. It is in the imagination that thought and desire fuse; and it is by means of the imagination that naturally arising tensions and contradictions are symbolically resolved. It is the imagination that invests what is otherwise humdrum – whether a person, a landscape or a quadratic equation – with almost magical significance. In no sense, in other words, is it optional, auxiliary or bolted on. If individuals are capable of thinking or relating in ways they find intrinsically rewarding, they are so on the strength of the energies that the imagination harnesses and turns to good account.

Our concluding chapters discuss in some detail the ways in which the imagination works. At this stage, there are three points to be made about it. These concern the categories fundamental to imaginative activity, the nature of the relevant intellectual operations, and the extent to which imaginative activity can transcend its origin in the infant/parent bond.

We see as fundamental two familiar pairs of categories:

Self and *other*; and

Similarity and *difference*.

The categories within each pair are mutually defining, of course; and, in practice, the two pairs are in complex ways semantically interlocked.

The most important of the intellectual operations brought to bear on these categories are the mind's ability:

To entertain *ambiguity* and *dissonance*; and

To displace emotionally charged preoccupations from the realm of the *literal* to that of the *symbolic*.

Initially, in infancy, these categories and operations are part-and-parcel of the infant/parent bond; but, as the individual matures:

The imagination becomes *autonomous*.

Progressively, it dissociates itself from its Oedipal roots and has a life of its own. The extent of this dissociation varies from individual to individual, being more pronounced in a mathematician, say, than in a poet, painter or psychologist. It follows that the middle-aged male mathematician imaginatively seized by a particular quadratic equation is not responding to distant memories of his mother or father. He is doing mathematics. Nevertheless, if the view adopted here is correct, his response to equations has the focus and driven force it does because his investments in his parents once took the form they did.

Together, these ideas about human development and the role of the imagination make up a mechanism, the theoretical equivalent of a piece of clockwork; and, left to its own devices, it will run and run. In doing so, it emphasises certain incompatibilities of perception and need that arise of their own accord between men and women. These are deep-rooted and pervasive, but they characteristically express themselves, we are going to argue, in terms of the fine rather than the coarse grain of human exchange.[3]

The Male Pattern

The male child separates himself in his imagination from his mother, we argued in *The Way Men Think*, and subsequently identifies himself with his father. By means of that identification, he becomes a person in principle dissimilar from the mother who afforded him primitive comfort, and akin to a creature he initially saw as alien or 'other': his father. To begin with, in other words, the small boy sees his mother as familiar, his father as alien. He then recognises his likeness to his father. He discovers, that is to say, similarity-in-difference. If he subsequently desires women, he desires creatures who belong to a category he once belonged to, but belongs to no longer. He thus enters into a dance or dialectic in which the detection of similarity-in-difference and difference-in-similarity are of poignant and enduring significance.

As a consequence of his separation from his mother, and the enduring sense of dislocation this causes – the male wound – boys will also suffer characteristic confusions or reversals. At root, these are ones in which, imaginatively speaking, people are treated as though they were objects, and objects as though they were people. From them, a pattern of typically 'male' strengths and weaknesses flows. This we described in detail in *The Way Men Think*.

Among the weaknesses, the most conspicuous are *personal insensitivity* – a failure to appreciate the nuances of human interaction and motive; and a distrust of the opposite sex that easily becomes *misogynous*. In compensation, there are advantages;

and in each, a point of disability is turned into a strength. Once accomplished, the boy's separation from his mother establishes in him not only a lingering dislocation but also a *sense of agency*; the knowledge that he can re-order the world in the light of his own imperious needs. He also has the capacity for *abstraction passion*, investing in the impersonal and mechanical those needs and energies that would otherwise be appropriate to an intimacy. In addition, the dissonances caused by his separation from his mother can serve him as a self-replenishing *energy source*. Resolutions of the dissonance created by the wound are symbolic; they do not – and cannot – reunite the boy symbiotically with his mother. However triumphant it seems at the time, each resolution sooner or later loses its lustre, and the search for a more definitive resolution begins again.

It follows from the events of early development in the male – his separation from the mother to whom he has been symbiotically linked, and his subsequent identification with the father who, until that point, has seemed alien – that some element of otherness (or, to use the Hegelian phrase, 'self-estrangement') is built into the developing male's sense of himself, and that an element of intimate familiarity lingers in what he sees as separate from himself or other.[4] For the male, that is to say, both self and other contain elements which are intimately familiar and also elements which are strange or alien. In a way that does not arise for his sister, the male is 'in' what he sees as other, and absent from what he sees as himself. As a consequence, we have claimed, the male imagination is typically:

Objectifying;

Passionate, in that it expresses powerful emotions of the kind which might otherwise be expressed in intimate relationships;

Binary, in that it falls naturally into the argumentative frameworks of conflict and reconciliation between opposed forces;

Subject to characteristic reversals, in which things are treated as though they were people, and people as though they were things; and

Activated, at root, by fantasies of purity, of control, of the penetration of mysteries, and of magical rediscovery and repossession.

This cast of mind expresses itself paradigmatically in disciplines like technology and physical science; in pursuits like the restoration of old railway engines and collecting postage stamps; in the purchase of sophisticated hardware; in computer games; in pin-ups and pornography. In as much as they strive for order, we envisage men doing so to reaffirm their sense of mastery and control. In the language of psychoanalysis, order serves the male as a defence; a bulwark that holds fantasies of isolation or engulfment at bay, and creates a space within which deeply serious games can be played – games in which formal intelligence and driven need merge.

What the male imagination offers, of course, are not literal representations of the world at large; still less, direct access to it. Rather, it generates working models of actuality; emotionally charged simulacra that can be adapted, should the need arise, to give a better fit with properties that the external world displays.

The Female Pattern

While lacking the qualities and quirks imparted to the male mind by the wound, the female imagination has distinguishing attributes of its own; some a source of strength, others more troublesome.

Unlike her brothers, the small girl need experience no dislocation in achieving a biologically appropriate gender identity. She can establish a sense of herself as female and at the same time remain symbiotically linked to her mother. If her expressions of desire as an adult reveal arbitrary reversals and paradoxes, they will be of a different order from those displayed by the male. For her, there need be no fantasies of magic repossession or return; none of the terror that too intimately symbiotic a connection so easily inspires in a man. For the woman, the most obvious danger of heterosexual love is that she will commit herself to a male who sees her, apparently quite arbitrarily, as infinitely attractive and infinitely alarming by turns.

It is often said of women that they live-in-relation, and the advantages of doing so are obvious.[5] In personal matters, such an individual is both perceptive and sympathetic. Intuitively receptive to subtleties of feeling and motive, she will cope naturally with certain emotionally demanding roles, especially perhaps those of care and nurture. In addition, if recent theorising is correct, she will be able to use her close relationships as a secure base from which to develop her own more impersonal accomplishments.[6]

The quality of mind characteristic of this typically female pattern is its *subjectivity*. Whatever is perceived as other – people, ideas, things – is gathered up and subordinated to the individual's wishes, the shape of this subordination depending on what her priorities happen at a given moment to be. If the wounded male characteristically has trouble in understanding that people are people, his sister has difficulty in grasping that other people – and, more generally, the world beyond the sovereign realm of her own desires – may be governed by priorities wholly unrelated to her own. For lack of a less Teutonic phrase, she finds difficulty in grasping the *otherness of the other*.

In contrast to the male, then, the female imagination will typically tend to be:

Intuitive, empathetic;

Unitary, in that principles and loyalties spontaneously govern actions;

Non-reflexive, in that its own quirks and perversities go unperceived and unacknowledged; and

Personal, in that, within it, the notion of the objective truth has no immediately graspable meaning.

Plainly, on the other hand, there are not only women who are formidably orderly; there are women who find themselves free to explore the external world on its own terms. They are so, we would argue, because objectivity serves them as a satisfactory defence against emotional – and, in origin, Oedipal – turbulence. Far from imposing their will on recalcitrant material, such women display both intuition towards their chosen slice of the natural order and also dispassion. As Evelyn Keller has pointed out, there are women scientists of distinction – she instances the Nobel Prize-winning geneticist Barbara McClintock – who 'listen to the material' and develop a 'feel' for it.[7] Another Nobel Prize winner,

Dorothy Hodgkin, fits Keller's argument well. Hodgkin has commented on the parallel between the crystallography she practised as an adult and her childhood experience of archaeology in Trans-Jordan with her parents. 'You're finding what's there and then trying to make sense of what you find,' she has said, 'you aren't controlling your situation.'[8]

The evidence of such scientists' lives suggests that women are disposed towards order in ways which differ from those moving men; and that, in practice, the performance of the two sexes will accordingly differ. Within a specific discipline – laboratory science, say, or macro-economics – women may find that their understanding of factual matters is clearer-eyed than that of their male colleagues, and less cluttered by *idées fixes*.

Mothers and Daughters as Rivals

There is another respect, however, in which patterns of development may be expected to generate sex differences among adults. It concerns the rewards and penalties of intimacy itself; and, thus, has a more immediate bearing on the path that close relations follow.

Beyond the question of their own separateness, the distinctive developmental task facing girls, as many commentators have pointed out, concerns not their gender identity but their object choice. They must establish a biologically appropriate focus for their desires. The small girl must transfer her desire from its original focus, her mother, to a new one, her father. In following this path, the female not only enters foreign territory, she does so intent on reestablishing with a man the symbiotic connection she once enjoyed with her mother.

In the nature of things, this undertaking is bound to fail. For this reason among others, the adult woman will be inclined to:

Regard her intimacies with other women as the only real intimacies; and

Remain narcissistically absorbed with her own body.

Where, in Carol Gilligan's words, men see danger in 'entrap-
ment or betrayal, being caught in a smothering relationship or
humiliated by rejection and deceit', women see danger in isolation
and in the fear of being left alone.[9] Gilligan concludes that 'men
and women may experience attachment and separation in different
ways', each sex perceiving a danger the other does not perceive –
'men in connection, women in separation'. The success of an intimacy between them depends not on their learning appropriate
physical manoeuvres with regard to one another's bodies, still less
on their adherence to fashionable, politically correct beliefs, but on
the mutual accommodation of systems of fantasied need and perception that are in principle incommensurable.

These difficulties have already been quite widely discussed.
There is, however, a less familiar feature of female development
which also deserves mention. If we are right, it is a potent source
of mutual incomprehension between the sexes, and has its point of
origin in the rivalry, fantasied or real, between the small girl and
her mother.

In agreement with many others, we see daughters as growing
up in relationships with their mothers which are characteristically
'undifferentiated and interdependent'; an arrangement which often
continues into adult life, and becomes the basis for 'the daughter's
relational mode as an adult'.[10] But in as much as she focuses her
desire on her father, the small girl wants what her mother wants –
or, at least, she wants what she imagines her mother wants; and
the two, rather than being symbiotically linked and united against
the world, become competitors. The daughter may wish not only
to muscle in on her mother's intimacy with her father, but to
usurp her mother in her father's eyes and monopolise his fascinated attention. Where this happens, the small girl loses her
mother as a source of primitive comfort, and exposes herself to
what she pictures as her mother's revenge.

Grant such highly charged ambivalences, and the chain of
implication becomes short:

In desiring her father, the daughter casts her mother in the role of
rival; and

In casting her mother as a rival, she activates the malign compo-
nents of the daughter/mother bond.

The daughter/mother bond is not only symbiotic; it is powerfully ambivalent, incorporating both the comforting and alarming, the good and bad. In as much as the small girl derives her sense of herself from the bond with her mother, her fantasies of her mother's anger will amplify her own. And because she has no means of distancing herself from this corrosive undertow of feeling, she will tend to 'export' bad feeling, imputing to others the feelings she finds alarming in herself, and thereby disowning them. As a result she will be more likely than her brothers to become preoccupied with issues of responsibility and blame.

As she cannot express her anger towards her mother without threatening her own identity, the small girl's anger will also tend to translate itself into depression. When she grows up, it is these ambivalences that close relationships with the opposite sex will reactivate. For women, in other words:

Heterosexual intimacy taps automatically into deep reservoirs of unresolved hostility, blame and depression.

How such daughter/mother rivalries work themselves out in practice will be influenced by the state of the small girl's relationships with her parents, and by the nature of the intimacy on which she wishes to intrude. There are fathers who love their wives and their daughters, and who keep these two relationships separate; the one eroticised, the other not. There are also fathers who are bored by their wives, delighted by their daughters, and eager to enter with their daughters into quasi-erotic (and sometimes forthrightly sexual) games. Similarly, while there are mothers who are protective towards their daughters and act in their best interests, there are also mothers who are rejecting; and ones who direct their love neither towards spouse nor daughter, but towards a son. But whatever the configuration, the hidden concomitant of the daughter's desire for her father will in all essentials be the same. Where heterosexual desire in the male promises a magical return to a state of primitive intimacy and connectedness, in the female it brings with it an incubus of identity-threatening anger and fathomless gloom. It does this in adolescence; and it does so again in adult love affairs and in marriage.[11]

There are clear predictions. The most obvious is that, as the statistical evidence confirms, depression among women is more closely associated than it is among men with love affairs and marriages that are going wrong.[12] Less obvious is the implication that women will be more likely than men to become depressed in marriages and intimacies *that are going well*. Again the statistical evidence is confirmatory: among the happily married, women are five times as likely to be depressed as men. A stock response to such a finding is that women are depressed by the historical injustices of their role. But without denying these injustices, our theory points in another direction. At such moments, it indicates, a significant source of a woman's discontent lies within herself.

Points of Departure, Points of Arrival

As we argued in *The Way Men Think*, the ways in which differences of psychological organisation find expression are typically complex; profound differences of underlying structure and motive often being surprisingly difficult to detect. The cerebral organisation of left- and right-handed people may differ in highly significant respects, for example, yet, in their everyday dealings with one another, these differences may play little or no part. The same principle applies in the field of sex and gender. The development of sex-linked patterns of thought and action is not a question of a single choice between 'male' and 'female', but of a series of such choices which interact:

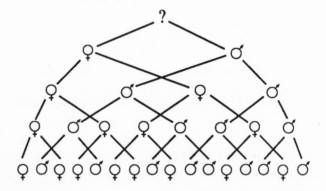

This diagram shows how, when arranged in series, the four basic divergences appropriate to an individual's sex and gender (biology, gender identity, object choice, and presentation of self) yield not two solutions but sixteen; each configuration a distinctively different resolution to the quandaries that sex and gender pose.[13] At the left and right extremes are individuals who conform to society's expectations of them: the woman who sees herself as a woman, desires men, and presents herself to the world as feminine; and the man who sees himself as a man, desires women, and presents himself to the world as masculine. In between, though, there is scope for diversity: the woman who sees herself as a man, desires other women, but presents herself to the world as feminine; the man who sees himself as a woman, desires women, and presents himself as effeminate; and so on. The complexity of these more elaborated solutions, produced under the pressure of ambivalence, is in principle limitless; and in practice is constrained only by the ingenuity of those driven to fashion them.

It is a further property of such lattice-like structures that adjacent destinations can be reached from widely differing points of departure. These dissimilarities are often so fine-drawn that the languages of psychology and of common sense collapse before them; yet they exert a formative influence on the sexes' perceptions of one another. The point is vital to our argument, and especially to a grasp of the way in which the biographical material in the next two chapters is organised. A recent advertising campaign provides an illustration.

Paris Lip

There exists a great deal of evidence to show that, in their sexual lives, men are fetishistic in ways which women are not.[14] It is tempting to go on to say that where men perceive the human body 'instrumentally', women view it 'transactionally'. In certain contexts, on the other hand, women are *more* likely than men to treat bodies – and, in particular, their own bodies – as objects. Advertisements for a form of cosmetic surgery – 'Paris Lip' – show how finely the responses of the two sexes are in this respect attuned. By means of four diagrams that would have done credit to the surrealist Max Ernst, the female reader is encouraged to perfect her pout, thus following in the footsteps of Madonna, Julia

Roberts and 'sexy' Michelle Pfeiffer. The first diagram shows collagen being injected by hypodermic needle along the line of the upper lip, adding definition. The second shows the needle accentuating the 'Cupid's Bow' with a distinctive 'V' shape. In the third, the needle accentuates the twin lines which lead up from the mouth to the nose, creating 'the distinctive peaks that are the signature of the Paris Lip'; while in the fourth, the needle adds weight to the lower lip, adding further definition and balancing the whole effect.

No doubt there are men who respond favourably to the thought of cosmetic surgery; but presumably there are few, the transsexual apart, who would do so to the advertisement for Paris Lip. Both explicitly and more covertly, its appeal is to women; yet the routine descriptive categories of the human sciences offer little help in making sense of such differences in susceptibility. Rather, we require theoretical frameworks which admit differences of principle, but allow these to be expressed, as in the decision tree, in terms of emotionally charged nuance.

In the field of sex and gender, it follows, *both* distinctions of principle *and* nuances are the psychologist's proper concern. Numerically overwhelming sex differences do sometimes arise, as, for instance, in recruitment to a discipline like quantity surveying, or in the incidence of specific sexual perversions like voyeurism and fetishism. But these are the exceptions. The normal case is the one in which men and women perform the same or closely analogous roles, but in which their performances are in detail dissimilar, and their experience, when examined closely, proves in significant respects to be mutually opaque. Nowhere are such discrepancies and opacities more evident than in close relationships between one sex and the other. Hence their theoretical fascination. And hence this book.

CHAPTER TWO

A Thought Experiment: Public and Private Lives

IN THIS CHAPTER AND the next, we use biographical vig-
nettes to explore the ways in which the thought processes of
the two sexes differ. The dissimilarities at issue, we believe, are
intuitively apparent to both sexes, but are often elusive and difficult to capture in words. In selecting lives to describe, we have
concentrated on women; and particularly on women who are
remarkable in that they have altered our view of society. We do
this in order to avoid the comparison, point by point, of male
and female lives – inescapably a long drawn out and inconclusive
affair – and because, in *The Way Men Think*, we have already published biographical accounts of remarkable men.

In place of any attempt to match the lives of samples of men
and women, and to draw conclusions from these comparisons, we
want to use biographical material to set up a *'thought experiment'* –
an investigation of the kind which can be conducted in the mind's
eye, and which, we hope, our readers will undertake on our
behalf. Although such manoeuvres have largely fallen into disuse
in the human sciences, there are signs that they are making a
return to favour. Where physicists use such mental experiments to
picture what the consequences of a certain practical intervention
could be, psychologists, sociologists and linguists more often use
them to tease out the assumptions implicit in everyday language or
behaviour.[1] Our thought – or *'Gedanken'* – experiment takes this
typically psychological form:

> We invite our readers to stop at any point in the next two chapters,
> and to envisage the sexes of the protagonists as reversed; the
> women as men, and the men as women.

Our predictions are that this gender-switch will usually be
achieved only with a sense of strain; and that it will be more difficult to perform the more the life in question is considered in

detail. More specifically, we predict that many of the episodes we describe will only make sense as events in the life of a man if circumstances are exceptional – if, for example, the man is envisaged as impersonating a woman, or as emotionally disturbed.

If our predictions are confirmed, which we believe they will be, the implication is that there exists a deeply engrained 'grammar' of sexual difference, which acts to ensure that some patterns of thought and action come more naturally to one sex than the other. The scene is then set for the arguments about the future of intimacy we want to make next. If, on the other hand, readers find the experiment's gender-switches either easy or impossibly difficult, the air of optimism surrounding those arguments is threatened. They would remain worth making, but the prospect they offer – of members of the two sexes finding it normal to live together in a state of enduring imaginative fertility – begins to fade. The imagination needs dissonance; and it withers in the face of differences that are either non-negotiable or so easily negotiated as scarcely to qualify as differences at all.

The materials for our thought experiment are gathered around two closely interconnected themes: the relation of the private person to the public person, of passion to action; and the question of veridicality, of telling the truth. As far as is practicable in a short space, we allow remarkable individuals' stories to tell themselves. We intervene, of course, especially when a puzzling or paradoxical feature would otherwise be lost from view.

A Household of Women

There were times in the 1960s and early 1970s when it seemed that Britain's first female prime minister would be Shirley Williams, Margaret Thatcher's Labour Party rival. She was one of 'those nice Labour moderates' Mrs Thatcher was later to castigate; an egalitarian by conviction and, in Hugo Young's phrase, 'a healer not a warrior by temperament'.[2]

There stood behind Williams a mother famous in her own right, Vera Brittain. Like her daughter and like Margaret Thatcher, Vera Brittain had been a student at Somerville College, Oxford. She served as a nurse during the First World War; and later recorded her experiences in *Testament of Youth*, an autobiographical best-seller that helped crystallise anti-war sentiment in Britain during the 1930s, and on which her reputation now depends.

Published in 1933, *Testament of Youth* was Vera Brittain's sixth book. There had previously been a book of verse, two novels, and two works of non-fiction: *Women's Work in Modern Britain* and *Halcyon, or The Future of Monogamy*. For ten years at least, the undertaking had hung fire; and when she eventually found the for-mat she needed, she did so in the context of child-birth and child-raising. Her first child John, was born in December 1927, a week before her thirty-fourth birthday. She at last settled to write *Testament of Youth* in November 1929, and, three weeks later, dis-covered that she was pregnant with Shirley – named, Vera insisted, after Charlotte Brontë's bold heroine, not after Shirley Temple. The text runs to quarter of a million words. In it, Vera describes her childhood, her experiences of the First World War, and her career up to the point of her marriage. It is a narrative strongly infused with war's horror and loss; and in it she puts traumatic memories to rest: the deaths, especially, of her younger brother Edward, and his close friend Roland Leighton, with whom she had been in love. It is an indictment of war, her biog-rapher Hilary Bailey observes, 'intended to bear witness to the past, to celebrate the dead and, perhaps, to exorcise her own pain'. 'It begins with peace and calm, is succeeded by crisis and disaster and ends with reconciliation.'[3]

Even with hindsight, however, it is easy to misunderstand quite what the nature of Vera Brittain's suffering was. When the war began, she was twenty; and to an extent that is nowadays scarcely credible, she was, like many of her contemporaries, jingoistic. On the other side, as timorous a figure as the German poet Rilke con-fessed to being in the grip of war fever too.[4] The day war began, Vera's diary records 'Today has been too exciting for me to feel at all like sleep – in fact it is one of the most thrilling I have ever lived through.'[5] She and her mother were eager that sensitive, musical young Edward should abandon his place at Oxford, and should volunteer without delay. Her father, on the other hand, was opposed; and, within the family, the row rumbled on for weeks. 'Daddy does not care about Edward's honour and cour-age,' Vera writes; and again, 'The morning opened in gloom, owing to Daddy's unconquerable aversion to Edward's doing any-thing for his country.' But in the end Edward went to war; and so did Roland. In 1915, Roland was killed; in 1916, Edward was seriously wounded in the Somme attack, returning to the front to be killed in 1918, five months before the war's end. In the Somme attack, Edward was awarded the Military Cross – for marching his troops at gun-point towards the German machine-gun fire. Even at this late stage, after Roland Leighton's death, and when Vera was working in military hospitals as a nurse, her responses were still those of a jingo. She was thrilled by Edward's decoration for bravery, yet jealous on Roland's behalf that it was Edward rather than he who would receive a hero's welcome at their old school, Uppingham.

Edward had gone to war 'roaring with laughter at Mother's anxiety on his behalf'. But, as must have become increasingly plain to Vera, it was not a laughing matter. He had gone to face death, under urgent pressure exerted in part by her. It was with this fact that, nearly twenty years later, she had to come to terms.

In 1925, Vera married George Catlin, an accomplished young Oxford academic who, while still in his twenties, had become pro-fessor of politics at Cornell. It was Vera's relationship with her fellow student Winifred Holtby, however, that was the pivot on which her life turned; and it was as much the unmarried Winifred as Vera herself who was responsible for bringing up John and Shirley. The future cabinet minister grew up in a household run by a pair of clever and intellectually productive women, mutually devoted, who pooled their resources in order to nurture the next generation.[6]

Winifred's health was poor. At one stage, she consulted a specialist who diagnosed Bright's Disease, and gave her two years to live. Vera's response to her friend's illness was not in the least what one might expect from someone with first-hand experience of nephritic patients: it seems that she asked Winifred few search-ing questions about her symptoms. There is something curious, too, about Vera's reaction to the absence of the convalescent Winifred. Vera invited Winifred's friend, the successful novelist Phyllis Bentley, to stay. Phyllis was installed in Winifred's room, and together she and Vera entered a round of fevered social activity. There were, Bailey relates, 'visits, dressings-up, exchanges of letters and presents, quarrels and reconciliations, all in the man-ner of teenage girls'. When Winifred returned briefly to the

London house, subject to a regime of early nights, plain food and injections, 'the door banged continually behind Vera and Phyllis, as the happy pair dressed in their best went out to yet another theatre or party'. Later, grotesque manoeuvrings were to surround Winifred as she lay mortally ill. Vera inveigled the man Winifred loved to propose to Winifred, the while vying with Winifred's mother to be the one at the death bed. Finally it was Vera who, having reached an understanding with the night sister, was sitting by Winifred's bed, holding her hand as, heavily sedated, she died.

Vera's strange responses to Winifred's illness arose, Bailey claims, because 'she cared too much and could not bear to hear the truth'. It is hard to avoid the impression, though, that there was something impersonal in Vera's need for Winifred. There is evidence of the same tendency in her dealings with men. When she came to write about the deaths of Roland Leighton and her brother, she could write about Roland's dry-eyed, but wept over Edward's. It is at least arguable that both her husband George and her lover Roland were surrogates for Edward. It is also arguable that the ambivalences she expiated in *Testament of Youth* were those she experienced as a child, loving her younger brother, but sufficiently jealous of him to embrace the war-mongering rhetoric of 'Death before Dishonour' that could only place him in mortal danger.

Sexual Politics

Kate Millett's *Sexual Politics* was published in 1970, the year Vera Brittain died.[7] An international best-seller, it was welcomed in one quarter as 'supremely entertaining, brilliantly conceived, overwhelming in its arguments, breathtaking in its command of history and literature'; in another as 'a book which must take its place at a single leap in the ranks of the best modern polemical literature'. In it, Millett used literature, history and psychoanalytic theory to propound a view now hackneyed but then startling in its simplicity. Both in our institutions and in our habits of thought we are patriarchal, she argued. The power of the male is used at every turn to exploit, devalue and disempower the female, the crucial instrument in this betrayal of one sex by the other being the family. If the corrupt and corrupting are swept aside, Millett's argument assumes, human beings will flourish, resplendent in their diversity.

Kate Millett became famous as a fiery advocate of feminism and civil rights, and while she married, she did so in a semi-detached style reminiscent of Vera Brittain's. Also like Brittain, she committed herself wholeheartedly to intimacies with other women; in particular, her friend Sophie Kerr. Unlike Brittain, she suffered protracted periods of mental instability which she was to describe, twenty years later, in *The Loony Bin Trip*.[8] During these periods, her confrontation with patriarchy became a confrontation with psychiatrists and nurses, and with those of her family and friends determined to incarcerate her.

The glib response to works like *Sexual Politics* is that their authors were acting out at society's expense the frustrations implicit in their relations with their fathers. A rider says that such acting out is especially vehement in those cases where the father neglects or rejects his daughter; where, as in Millett's case, the father abandons wife and children and sets up a new family elsewhere. On this argument, militant feminism is a response both to the Oedipal pressures inherent in the father/daughter relationship, and to broken homes. What *The Loony Bin Trip* inadvertently establishes is that this glib response is in Millett's case accurate. It is a narrative which unfolds like a malicious invention, devised by a male chauvinist to discredit Millett's political views.

Kate Millett's account of herself in *The Loony Bin Trip* is unbridled; it is also insistently *genital*. At one point, she describes her actress sister as announcing to the womenfolk of the family, 'I love it, I just love cock.'[9] In evoking her intimacies with Sophie Kerr she is equally outspoken: 'We were unable to stop, one gratification only calling for another, the wildest improvisations, the never-finished copulation, franker and more animal than with any lover I'd ever known. Fond of the same pleasures, fond of all pleasures, an infinite variety of subtle clitoral stimulation, hard vaginal fucking, anal invention, breasts, eyes, the never-satisfied mouth; how easy and endless the going down, the coming up to rest on a nipple or a kiss or a look – the highest trust, the secret between us, the billy goat lust of our perfect shamelessness, all borders passed, transcended – utterly given to each other, in league.'[10] Such outpourings are startling in their own right; but strangely reminiscent, too, of the purple passages in Henry Miller's work – material of a kind that Millett had been at such pains to discredit in *Sexual Politics*.

More specifically, she describes her realisation that, all along, she has been obsessed with her father, and that the nature of that obsession is incestuous. An attractive Irishman, her father deserted wife and three daughters in St Paul, Minnesota, remarried and had another family. Decades later, Kate, the middle daughter, was to buy a horse for her Poughkeepsie farm – a gelding – and name it after her father. 'Are you here to remind me', she asks, 'wonderful obscene presence, to recall that modest man I lusted after in childhood? An adolescent dying of curiosity about the wonder between his legs, hidden by custom, gentlemanly and pointless custom, whose effect was only further curiosity, mystification. Having missed sight of my father's red genitals, an inch glimpsed between the folds of his shorts as he changed clothes before his bath, after a day building roads, have I found again in your grand black dangling cock something of the hero in that tired man? – that force, that aging grandeur, that prizefighter's fatigue, that exhausted athlete.'[11] 'Touching it', she believes, 'would be to connect with the last taboo, past bestiality to incest: utopian prehistorical world. The Amazon's perfect freedom within the pleasure principle.'[12] 'Tonight in this moonlight, though, it is for me alone Jim hangs down his cock, to let me touch its alien velvet, really quite afraid of him and his size, of the taboo and the forbidden, of my own adoring lust before this amazement.'[13]

As Millett herself observes, she has written a whole book against patriarchy, yet 'on a little hillock in a field by moonlight I communicate with you through a horse ... to touch this great wonderful cock is to touch all maleness, beloved and tender, heroic and other and still the same, because joined in the very meat we are all made of ...'.[14] In writing this Lawrentian passage, Millett seems only partially to realise that she is cutting away the ground on which she stood as a young radical; or, if she realises it, she seems no longer to care. Not only does she undermine the feminist critiques of patriarchy and 'phallocentricity'; she supplies autobiographical chapter and verse for the argument which says that such critiques derive their fuelling charge from Oedipal forces inadequately transmuted or repressed. The implication must be that while *Sexual Politics* purported to be a book against patriarchy, it was in fact a book against its author's father; one she wrote

in order to hold her disappointed longing for him within manageable bounds.

The Patriarch's Daughter

In the year that Vera Brittain died and Kate Millett published
Sexual Politics, Margaret Thatcher was beginning her career as a
cabinet minister. Five years later, she was leader of the opposition;
and within four more she was prime minister. She was the first
woman to hold the post; she was the first British prime minister to
have been trained in the natural sciences; and she was to remain in
power longer than anyone in modern times.[15] Typically, the prime
ministership is a role that exhausts its incumbents, but in this
respect, too, she was exceptional. As Penny Junor, one of her
biographers says, 'she works a seven-day week and, regularly, a
nineteen- or twenty-hour day. She has few friends, no hobbies
and, with the possible exception of her family, no interest in anything outside politics.'[16] It is the kind of regime that puts 'strong
men into basket chairs'. Yet, while in office, her performance grew
progressively more convincing rather than less. By her third term,
the shrill zealot of her early years had been transformed into the
quasi-mythical figure of Gloriana Imperatrix.

The Thatcher background was humble: her paternal grandfather
a cobbler, her maternal grandfather a cloakroom attendant on the
railway.[17] Her father, Alfred Roberts, was a self-made man who
left school at thirteen. He had gone into the grocery business, subsequently buying a shop of his own in a slummy district of
Grantham. His two daughters were born above the shop, and, as
Hugo Young observes, 'it is from this place, and the upright
patriarch who presided over it, that many lessons were learned
which touched the governance of Britain fifty years later'.[18] Alfred,
a strict Methodist and later alderman and mayor, expounded the
Victorian values of hard work, self-help and careful budgeting. He
also had the Victorian passion for education; the key, he believed,
to a full and useful life. Margaret's mother was a seamstress by
training, by all accounts a devoted but down-trodden figure. Also
of the household was Margaret's sanctimonious maternal grandmother Phoebe.

Although outnumbered by his womenfolk by four to one, it was Alfred's presence that was dominant: 'a paragon among political parents, an influence acknowledged with repeated and explicit reverence by his daughter throughout years when other political leaders might have been pleased to see their present achievements obliterate their past'.[19] In contrast, the female side of Margaret Thatcher's family – mother, grandmother, older sister – seems to have been of more purely personal significance to her. She makes no mention of her mother in her entry in *Who's Who*; and if pressed by interviewers in later years, would refer to her dismissively as something of a Martha. In Charles Rycroft's helpful phrase, her female kin seem to have been ablated from the future prime minister's sense of herself as a public being.[20] As a politician, she was also conspicuously chary of letting competent women anywhere near her.

The Roberts' house lacked an inside lavatory and running hot water; the result not so much of poverty as of 'thrift carried to the point of parsimony'. Baths were taken once a week, in the warehouse behind the shop. The household boasted a piano, and when Margaret was ten, it acquired a radio; but, as children, she and her older sister Muriel had few possessions, fewer fripperies. The household was also strictly Sabbatarian, Margaret and Muriel being forbidden to play on Sunday, even to sew or knit. Each Sunday, the two girls put in four appearances at the Methodist church in the centre of Grantham where their father preached, and from which he would set out, in his mature years, to deliver the Methodist message to the surrounding villages. For the girls, there was Sunday school at 10.00am, morning service at 11.00am, Sunday school again at 2.30pm, at which Margaret sometimes played the piano, and finally evening service at 6.00pm. From an early age, Margaret not only had piano lessons but compulsory library visits, her contemporaries remembering her for her 'bulging satchel and earnest questioning in class'.

At Somerville, Margaret chose to read chemistry. She worked hard, and in her fourth year acted as assistant to Dorothy Hodgkin, who was later to say kind words about her. 'I came to rate her as good,' Hodgkin once observed. 'One could always rely on her producing a sensible, well-read essay.'[21] Having graduated, Margaret went to work in 1947 as an industrial chemist, first for a firm in Essex called British Xylonite Plastics, who made spectacle frames and other household goods; and then in the research department of J. Lyons, testing cake-fillings and ice-cream. But her mind was already focused elsewhere. From the outset, she had revealed a passionate, unbending, and in those days most unusual commitment to the politics of the Conservative Party.

In 1951, she married Denis Thatcher. His wealth freed her from the need to earn a living as a chemist and allowed her to study for the bar. Denis had inherited a family business, begun by a grand-father who made weed-killer and sheep-dip, and which subsequently expanded into the manufacture of paint and other chemicals. When, in 1965, the Atlas Preservative Company was taken over by Castrol, Denis became rich; and when Castrol was in turn taken over by Burmah Oil, he joined the board of a major international enterprise, with a Daimler and later a Rolls Royce to match. His retirement at the age of sixty coincided almost exactly with the point at which his wife's career as a major political figure took off, and he lent her unwavering support. When she travelled, he travelled – always, as he wryly remarked, half a step behind. Although not himself political, everything he felt and thought, 'from staunch hostility to socialists and trade unions, through his no-nonsense approach to business accountancy, to his inextin-guishable affection for white South Africa' played their part in the 'ceaseless struggle between gut instinct and political calculation which became so prominent among the motifs threading them-selves through her prime ministership'.[22]

As a barrister, Margaret specialised in tax law. On and off, she practised for some five years; and although she had the usual diffi-culties associated with the career of a professional woman in a male preserve, these seemed to leave few scars. Interestingly, she chose a branch of the law which involved little court work and no appearances before a jury. There, 'without ever being more than a pedestrian lawyer', she developed a head for detailed numerical argument; a quality she was to display in her maiden speech as an MP.[23] Introducing a private member's bill on the right of access of the press to meetings of local councils, she spoke for twenty-seven minutes, furnishing apposite statistics, and did so with barely a reference to notes.

Already evident in her performance was the 'piercing' quality that was to become her hallmark as a politician; this allied to a passion for personal dominance and control. Exceptionally aggres-sive in debate, she hectored the opposition and did so irrespective of its grandeur. As prime minister, she became famous for achievements seen, stereotypically, as masculine. She won the Falklands War. She displayed sang-froid amid the rubble of the Brighton bombing. And, in many ways most telling, she tackled the trade unions. Where stout men had faltered and the governments of Heath and Callaghan had fallen, Margaret Thatcher's cabinet broke the miners' strike, sapping the influence, until then little short of mesmeric, of their leader Arthur Scargill. It would be the clumsiest of errors to assume, however, that because she performed feats that many men envied, she offered herself to the world as a species of man.

As her choice of name when in power indicates – 'Mrs', 'Margaret' or even 'Maggie Thatcher', rather than 'Ms', 'Margaret' or 'Maggie Roberts' – she was conventionally married, and at pains to seem so. While bossy towards her husband, she made it plain that she drew comfort and strength from him. 'When I'm in a state', she told a reporter soon after she first became prime minister, 'I have no one to turn to except Denis. He puts his arm round me and says, "Darling, you sound just like Harold Wilson." And then I always laugh.'[24] Her twin children were also important to her. Mark and Carol were brought up by a full-time nanny, and their mother saw relatively little of them. She also treated them formally ('dear' rather than 'darling'); but she was to become a devoted mother, even besotted, shedding tears in public when Mark was missing on a safari motor rally.

At the domestic level, she had picked up many of her mother's dress-making skills, sewing clothes for her children, and, on occasion, altering for her own use clothes passed down to her by Muriel. And she showed, throughout her married life, a zeal for home decorating; doing the stripping, painting and wall-papering herself, and to competent effect. Among her other qualities is a formidable facility with names. In the course of her adoption as parliamentary candidate in Finchley, Junor relates, she volunteered to Dutch auction a bottle of whisky from the bar. In a roomful of people whom she had met for the first time that evening, she called out their names in turn, and to general astonishment, did so without a mistake.[25]

Mrs Thatcher also chose to reveal a preoccupation with her complexion and her clothes. On a memorable occasion, she agreed to show her wardrobe on television to the viewing masses; and having arranged a rack of her favourite garments for the BBC's cameras, went through them with every appearance of innocent pleasure. Not only did she advise in favour of blue and black and against frills; she expounded the traditional virtues of the stitch in time that saves nine. Her underclothes, she firmly averred, came from that very British store Marks & Spencer. While such manoeuvres were undertaken on the advice of experts concerned to soften her image as the Iron Lady, what she revealed of herself was nonetheless convincingly direct.

Early in her career, there were many critics who portrayed Margaret Thatcher as a chilly woman who used her Low Church rhetoric as a weapon with which to carve through sensibilities frailer or more exotic than her own. Marina Warner suggested that she was flinty precisely in order to demonstrate that 'she is not under the governance of Venus, that she is a stranger to the exactions and weaknesses of the heart, that her most private organ is her gut'.[26] But although apposite at the time, this analysis became less apt as the Thatcher career unfolded. As a student, there evidently *was* something about her that peers regarded as cold, opportunistic and driven. A contemporary, Nina Bawden, speaks of her as 'a plump, pale, solemn girl of 19', who smiled her 'pretty china doll's smile'.[27] It is a perception that even her father seems sneakingly to have shared. 'Margaret is ninety-nine point five per cent perfect', he is once said to have said, 'the half per cent is that she could be a little bit warmer'.[28] Weighing against this is her reputation among those close to her for being both loyal and kind. She has been described as 'equitable, fair, and, above all, immensely appreciative' of the work others do for her, male and female alike.[29]

Although doubtless embroidered in the telling, two stories about Margaret Thatcher and food capture the complexity of her attitude to workmates: solicitous to those without power, brutal towards potential rivals. The first is related as fact by Junor; the second has more the status of a joke. The prime minister's official residence in the country, Chequers, is run by the military. One Sunday, Mrs Thatcher was entertaining members of her cabinet to lunch. A Wren, advancing with a serving dish of roast lamb and gravy, lost her grip and tipped lamb and gravy into the lap of Sir Geoffrey Howe, the chancellor of the exchequer. 'Margaret leapt to her feet, rushed to the scene of the disaster, put a comforting arm straight round the panic-stricken girl's shoulder and marched her out to the kitchen, saying there was nothing in the world to worry about, leaving Sir Geoffrey to mop up his suit himself.'[30] The significance of the story is two-fold: the prime minister's spontaneous solicitude towards someone whom she regarded as helpless; and the ruthlessness of her disregard for a male colleague who had been undeviatingly loyal to her, but whom, for personal reasons, she could not bear.

The second story also places the prime minister at the meal table with the members of her cabinet. 'I'll have steak,' she tells the waiter. 'And what about the vegetables?' he asks. 'Oh,' she answers, 'they'll have steak too.' Arguably, the kindliness of the first story and the brutality of both are part of a collective myth about the nature of politicians. On the other hand, the weight of anecdotal evidence indicates that these are as much features of the real Margaret Thatcher as is her commitment to her clothes and complexion.

Quirks and Contradictions

As a political performance, Mrs Thatcher's when in power was perhaps the most remarkable of her era; and, increasingly, it came to seem the natural outgrowth of her background and personality. There was, she claimed on the day she entered 10 Downing Street as prime minister, an unbroken link between the values her father had instilled in her and the message that had carried her to victory. Nevertheless, it was a performance shot through with paradox and contradiction; and the more closely it is examined, the stronger that impression becomes. Her faith in market forces, and her policies of deregulation and privatisation were certainly compatible with her father's political beliefs, which were those of an old-fashioned *laissez-faire* liberal. On the other hand, her attack on the 'nanny state' began only once she was in power. As secretary of state for education and science she had been a high spender; as was her fellow radical Keith Joseph, at the department of housing and local government. Her abolition of free school milk was not the draconian measure it was made to seem; rather, a trap prepared for her by hostile and embattled officials, into which she obligingly tumbled. Even when in place, the policies of her mature years were paradoxical in their effect. For the men and women whose interests these policies served were property developers, financial manipulators, entrepreneurs; many of them fleet of foot and some of them flamboyantly dishonest. Unless his was a more complex character than we realise, Margaret's high-minded father would have turned in his grave.[31]

Of her more specific quirks, two are startling. Throughout her career, Mrs Thatcher placed special trust in apostates; men who had political pasts that were grossly ideologically unacceptable to her, but which they had since renounced. Her first guru, before she took office as prime minister, was the right-wing journalist Alfred Sherman, who had once been a communist. Her press secretary and close working partner, Bernard Ingham, was a man with a career behind him as a Labour Party activist. John Vaizey, too, had been ennobled by the Labour prime minister Harold Wilson as recently as 1976, but had since defected to the Conservatives and become a friend. It is tempting to explain this taste for men with unacceptable pasts as congruent with her view of herself as an outsider; but there is a further possibility. Namely that many women, and especially perhaps those brought up in a context of remorseless high-mindedness, are magnetically drawn to men who have sinned but subsequently repented; a tendency as strong in the sexual sphere as in the social, and stemming from the equation of excitement with the forbidden.

The second quirk is, if anything, even more remarkable. It concerns Mrs Thatcher's method of choosing her right-hand men. In someone apparently so thorough and so controlling, this was little short of bizarre. As Young observes, her attitude 'was shot through with a paradox perhaps only explicable by feminine intuition. For although she set great store by individual character, and delighted in the personal loyalty of those closest to her, she took exceptionally little trouble to find out what they might really be like. Her most successful officials have always been those who developed an almost chemical empathy with her, not least as man to woman.'[32] But their selection was largely left to chance. Bernard Ingham's appointment as her press secretary was in this respect typical. A gritty north-countryman, Ingham was by training a press officer who had become an administrative civil servant. Soon after Mrs Thatcher became prime minister, he was summoned to Downing Street; and felt that, if offered the post of press secretary, he might well turn it down. But, straightaway, she spoke as if her offer and his acceptance were formalities already completed, and began to instruct him on how his new task should be performed. 'If she had ever caught sight of him before', Young claims, 'it could only have been through covert glances on her visit to his department. Yet in this fortuitous manner, devoid of the normal processes of rational choice, began one of the great enduring partnerships – as consistently close as she had with any other man – of Mrs Thatcher's years as Prime Minister.'[33]

Again, there are two interpretations. The first is that, at some quite primitive level, she must have intuited that their personalities were compatible; a judgement that could perhaps be made within seconds. As she once said to him after a bruising press conference, 'The thing about you and me, Bernard, is that neither of us are *smooth* people.' The second interpretation is complementary but different. Namely that Mrs Thatcher was someone in whom the chemistry of personal bonding with men was especially important; and that the operation of this chemistry was actually heightened by the element of randomness in her processes of selection. By analogy, some women respond sexually to strangers in ways that they cannot to intimates or friends. Some may even be impelled towards randomness, intuiting that the keenest excitements arise where rational choice has been abandoned.

Junor comments that Margaret Thatcher 'enjoys men finding her sexy, although she is far too entrenched in her Victorian morality ever to admit it. The men she likes are those that flirt with her. She likes extraverts, she likes people like Gordon Reece who look her straight in the eyes, laugh at her, and pat her on the hand. She enjoys the irreverence of someone like Ronnie Millar, who tells her she has the best cheek-bones in the business, but the lousiest hair-do.' The flirtation is never overt, Junor insists; there is never a question of a pass. It is the *frisson* that Mrs Thatcher enjoys: 'When she feels this mutual attraction, she is warm, relaxed and even at times, quite witty. If the feeling is absent, she can be like an ice-box. "She is like a matron telling you off for wetting the bed," said one who knows.'[34]

The vision of Margaret Thatcher as prime minister, in full possession of power, was, of course, painstakingly *constructed*: even such details, for example, as her accent and enunciation. To the native-born, these sound contrived; and they prove to be the

hybrid product of her Lincolnshire upbringing, of elocution lessons arranged for her by her father before she went to Oxford, and
of voice training many years later, designed to make her less shrill.
Even her fabled toughness was taught and learnt. The successful
prosecution of the Falklands War was the turning point in her for-
tunes, yet here too she needed and accepted advice. In the early
days of this venture, her resolution deserted her. Junor records
that 'She spoke at twice her normal pace. "What are we going to
do?" she would say, "what can we do for these people? Oh dear,
oh dear, oh dear, I do hope they're all right ... do you think
they're all right?"' It was Willie Whitelaw who took her aside and
explained that generals must be able to detect in their political
masters no trace of doubt. From that moment on, Junor claims,
she was 'utterly steadfast'.[35]

Subsequently, she took the advice not only of fellow politicians,
but of a retinue of public relations experts and theatre folk. Yet in
fashioning Gloriana Imperatrix, these professionals seem not to
have invented. They used personal qualities which were genuinely
Margaret Thatcher's, but which she had to be schooled to project.
At the same time, access to the medium of television and to power
itself seemed to release in her a previously hidden persona; and it
was of this new self that, in her mature years, Margaret Thatcher
gave a performance which was both deeply felt and manifestly
ham. There were occasions, as a consequence, when she seemed
less a person than the embodiment of a myth.

Unlikely though this may seem to many of her fellow Britons,
Mrs Thatcher's resolute public image came as a result to embody
not only political power but sexual allure.[36] French commentators
have been particularly eloquent in this respect. *Le Figaro*'s male
interviewer spoke of emerging from Downing Street with the
sense of a woman 'full of charm and seduction whose radiating
presence conceals a great authority and a deep-seated desire to
infuse some warmth into the climate of Franco-British relations'.
Le Quotidien de Paris rejected the thought of her as the Iron Lady.
Rather, she was a creature of uranium. 'Compared to her, how
leaden appear most of our leaders, opaque masses of flesh, austere
fortresses without windows...' Perhaps the most memorable of
these Gallic apperceptions, though, was to come from a fellow
politician; one completely out of sympathy with her beliefs. In
briefing his new European minister Roland Dumas about Mrs

Thatcher, President Mitterrand reputedly warned him, '*Elle a les yeux de Caligule, mais elle a la bouche de Marilyn Monroe.*' It is a conjunction designed to remind us that there are women who exercise power without stirring from the centre of their beings. It also conveys a hint: that there were moments when Margaret Thatcher's gaze, like that of the Roman emperor who raised his horse to the consulship, could sometimes seem to reflect the light of unreason.[37]

CHAPTER THREE

The Thought Experiment Continued: Telling the Truth

MARGARET MEAD WAS BORN in Philadelphia in 1901. She was thus eight years younger than Vera Brittain, but old enough to be Margaret Thatcher's mother. Both her parents were earnest academics. Her mother studied the families of Italian immigrants; her father read Veblen, and travelled the state, setting up extensions for the University of Pennsylvania.[1] Before she knew what the words meant, Margaret had learnt to say 'in one long difficult utterance: "My-father-majored-in-economics-and-minored-in-sociology-and-my-mother-majored-in-sociology-and-minored-in-economics."'[2] Her story touches on many of the issues raised by those of Vera Brittain, Kate Millett and Margaret Thatcher, but we have selected one aspect of her working life which sets it apart: that of *veridicality* – of making factual claims that are well-grounded.

The Most Famous Anthropologist in the World

Margaret Mead achieved fame rather in the sense that Benjamin Spock achieved it. Not only did hers become a household name; like Spock, she propounded a view of life – and, more specifically, of family life – accepted as enlightened by liberal-minded people throughout the Western world. She had the 'mantle of omniscience' thrust upon her, and wore it with panache. 'Margaret loved being in the public eye', a professional friend would say in retrospect, 'she loved being famous; she absolutely loved it.'[3] Her fame was such that, when she was seventy-five, a full-page advertisement appeared in the *New York Times* wishing her a happy birthday.[4]

Mead's role in the public imagination was inseparable from the impact of her first book. Published in 1928 while its author was still in her twenties, this became a best-seller. At the behest of her professor at Columbia, Franz Boas, she had done fieldwork among the Samoans; and in *Coming of Age in Samoa*, she describes the girls she observed there as free from many of the constraints taken for granted in Western society, and free, particularly, to enjoy sex. In Samoan society, she claimed, sex was a natural function, devoid of any notion of 'romantic love as it occurs in our civilization, inextricably bound up with ideas of monogamy, exclusiveness, jealousy and undeviating fidelity'. Adolescence, for the girls of Samoa, 'represented no period of crisis or stress, but was instead an orderly development of a set of slowly maturing interests and activities'. They wished to live with 'many lovers as long as possible and then to marry in one's own village, near one's own relatives, and to have many children'.[5]

Not only did free-thinking Western readers warm to such a vision; they were alert, many of them, to its ideological implication. As her biographer Jane Howard says, it seemed that there were 'ways and ways' not only of getting through puberty but of doing almost anything; that it was culture rather than biology that determined the path each person trod. This prospect was itself seen as an emancipation, for while biology was assumed to deny individuals their freedom, culture was believed to give them choice.

First born, Margaret was the focus of the family's attention, especially that of her adoring paternal grandmother, who treated her as a confidante. She learnt, too, from her mother and grandmother the 'rule of absolute solidarity among women'.[6] She grew up craving more companionship than any one person or family could provide; and she was to develop on the strength of this craving a formidable gift for friendship. By the time she was a student at Barnard, she had evolved her three rules for getting on with people: '(1) be useful to them; (2) be amusing for them; and (3) build them up in their own estimation'.[7] Later, she was to develop a reputation for being both witty and wonderfully exhilarating company, especially in the small doses that a tight-packed schedule of professional commitments allowed. Throughout her life she created 'families' from among colleagues and friends. She made, she estimated, 'an average of one new friend of importance every two or three months', and she shed few.⁸ Similarly with her relatives; far from drifting apart from former in-laws and distant cousins, she 'energetically sought them out, demanding to know how time was treating them'.⁹

Margaret Mead was – and remained throughout her life – headstrong, rash; and saw herself as a free spirit. She also had qualities which were forthrightly unpleasant, and which seem to have hardened with age. In her mature years, she was – to use her collaborator Ken Heyman's phrases – both a 'busybody' and a 'tough bitch'. At New York's Museum of Natural History, which was to become her professional home, she was considered formidable. 'Before I went to work for her there', one employee said, 'I was warned that I would probably have a nervous breakdown, and it was easy to see why. Doors would slam, secretaries would weep, often there was someone in the hallways sobbing.'¹⁰ The large majority of those who sobbed were unquestioningly loyal, though; and, in however menial a capacity, were only too happy to serve. As she grew older, Mead's toughness turned into bullying. To one of her victims, a female novelist who had had the temerity to criticise the United Nations, she gave the impression of 'a woman carried away with ambition and aggression, and pounding her way with brute force'. Calculation, this victim believed, had played a fundamental role in Mead's rise to prominence, and her egotism was ungovernable.¹¹ As a male colleague at Columbia once remarked, 'Margaret Mead was not the victim, ever, of anything.'¹²

She craved not only attention but fame. As her friend and mentor Ruth Benedick was to say, 'She isn't planning to be the best anthropologist, but she *is* planning to be the most famous.'¹³ Fuelling this concatenation of gifts and frailties was an astonishing vitality, which seems rarely to have flagged. 'It was almost a principle of pure energy,' Gregory Bateson, one of her husbands, was to say. 'I couldn't keep up, and she couldn't stop. She was like a tugboat. She could sit down and write three thousand words by eleven o'clock in the morning, and spend the rest of the day working at the museum.'¹⁴ With the passage of time, this drive became if anything more pronounced; a celebration, as she herself would proclaim, of 'post-menopausal zest'. In someone physically frail, it was a capacity fuelled, Jane Howard believes, by a horror of being alone and with nothing to do.

Often assumed to be a lesbian, Margaret was to marry three times. First, when twenty-one, she married Luther Cressman, soon to be ordained as a priest, and later to leave the clergy for archaeology. This marriage she would subsequently refer to as her 'student marriage', removing mention of it from her entry in biographical sources like *Who's Who*. Her engagement to Cressman, Howard suggests, 'proved to the world that she was a female desired by men'. More important, as Mead was herself to say, it 'gave me time for deep, creative friendships with women'.[15] Later, she was to marry first one fellow anthropologist and then another: the New Zealander Reo Fortune and Bateson, an Englishman. In each, she sought a working companion. It seems that she was deeply attached to Bateson, the father of her only child, and that she was mortified when he left her. But over both men she rode roughshod. A fellow anthropologist recalled seeing Mead and Bateson 'walking down the enormously long fifth-floor corridor of the Natural History Museum, with Margaret always two steps ahead of Gregory and talking like sixty, her hands going like mad – she always talked with her hands as well as her voice. She took two steps to every one of Gregory's. He was behind her, very quietly nodding and agreeing, but she never looked back . . .'[16]

At one point, Bateson taught a course in anthropological theory at the New School of Social Research. A student recalls him as 'tall and awkward and shy, without any stage presence'. Soon, Mead 'came to the class and sat in the middle of the middle aisle of seats, squarely facing her husband. As Bateson struggled through his lecture, Mead would rise dramatically from her seat and correct him on a minor point. "No Gregory", she would say, "it was not *that* way at all. It was *this* way . . ." and then go on to explain in her wonderfully crystal-clear manner.' This went on for two more weeks. Mead then took over the class, and Bateson was no more to be seen.[17] As the psychoanalyst Rollo May noticed, 'she would swing her broadsword and clip off ears and *then* communicate'.[18] Her high-handedness was a quality that Mead took with her when she went into the field. In the 1950s, she required her two assistants to photograph the inhabitants of a New Guinea village naked, both front view and in profile, because she was at that time interested in the relation of body-build to temperament. The villagers were mortified, and Mead's assistants were mortified; but the photographs were taken nonetheless.

It was relatively late in life that Mead became a mother, her daughter being born when she was thirty-eight. The previous afternoon, Margaret had finished writing an article for the *Encyclopaedia Britannica*, just as her own mother had finished writing an article for the *Encyclopaedia Britannica* before giving birth to her. But in Margaret's case there was the kind of commotion she found it second nature to create. Howard describes the delivery as being 'delayed for ten minutes until the arrival of the photographer'. It was 'witnessed by the obstetrician, several nurses (all of whom, at Mead's request, had seen the Bateson-Mead film "First days in the Life of a New Guinea Baby"), a child development psychologist, a movie photographer, and the pediatrician Dr. Benjamin Spock'. Significantly the father, Bateson, was elsewhere.[19]

The Mead Fiasco

Mead's fame spread. She became America's best-known scientist; and she moved from one gathering of luminaries to another, sporting the cloak and stave which became her trademark. The while, however, doubts were being expressed about the quality of her fieldwork. The data she had collected, alone in Samoa and later with Fortune in New Guinea, were, certain of her academic colleagues came to believe, suspect. Fortune said little, but it became clear that he disagreed flatly with his former wife's reading of the evidence they had gathered together.[20] Over the decades, this uneasiness grew. When, in the late 1960s, one of us (LH) was teaching social psychology to the archaeology and anthropology students at Cambridge, they appeared to take it for granted that Mead's fieldwork was unsound; but their response was more amused than hostile. To them it was mildly comic but intellectually telling that, once divorced, Mead and Fortune should differ sharply about what they had seen together in the field. This divergence, after all, was itself evidence of the sociological view of knowledge that Mead had done so much to consolidate, in which social relationships and systems of belief govern the perception of fact, not vice versa. While X is married to Y, X and Y perceive the world – and especially the world of sex and gender – within the frame of reference that their marriage creates. These perceptions will necessarily change for both X and Y if they then subsequently divorce.

Initially, the case against Mead was that her fieldwork had been impressionistic; that she had told the stories she needed to tell, not those the ethnographic evidence could properly be said to support. In the nineteenth century, writers like Robert Louis Stevenson had spoken of Samoa as a land of 'fine clean emotions; a world all and always beautiful'. It was this idealised and literary view that *Coming of Age in Samoa* seemed to reproduce; what was all and always beautiful being translated there into a vision of adolescence as a paradise, in which sex was both promiscuous and anxiety-free.[21]

In the years since her death in 1978 the case against Mead has hardened. Criticism first came sharply into focus in Derek Freeman's *Margaret Mead and Samoa, the Making and Unmaking of an Anthropological Myth*, published in 1983.[22] More recently still, suspicions of shoddy scholarship have been compounded by evidence that, in her questioning of the young women of Samoa, Mead had allowed herself to be duped. The claims now made against Mead are that her fieldwork in Samoa was brief and sketchy; that her interpretation of her own data obeyed the ground rules of polemic, not scholarship; and that she ignored contrary evidence about Samoan culture, collected not only by other anthropologists but also by herself. More specifically still, it is claimed that her two key informants – young women whom she had befriended, Fa'apua'a and Fofoa – engaged in 'recreational lying', a practice common in Samoa; and that she was hoodwinked. When she pressed them for information about their sex lives, they took refuge in a hoax. Rather than portray their adolescent attitudes towards sex in their true light – as somewhat strait-laced – they pretended to behaviour which was blithely libidinous.[23]

There is a good deal to be said in Margaret Mead's defence. When she went to Samoa in 1925, she was young, and, for most practical purposes of anthropological fieldwork, untrained. She had to gather what little help she could from fellow anthropologists she met *en route*, and via long-delayed letters from her mentor Boas. Her command of the language, too, was less than complete. What she confronted was a culture far from 'savage'; the influences of the American navy and the London Missionary Society being both strong and pervasive. The Society, particularly,

had been the dominant religious and educational presence on the
islands for the previous hundred years, and its teaching was
restrictive, especially with regard to adolescent girls, many of
whom lived under supervision in the pastor's home. Intellectually,
Margaret was unequipped to cope with the task of teasing apart
the original Samoan culture from the Western one imposed upon
it. As a result, her conclusions are inconsistent. At one point, in a
report to Boas, she claims that while the pagan religion of the area
had disappeared without trace, Samoan culture nonetheless had at
its centre a form of institutionalised virginity that was 'still vividly
alive'.[24] Yet in *Coming of Age in Samoa*, she explains the 'moral
premium on chastity' in terms of the Christian influence, and
the Samoan attitude towards it as one of 'reverent but complete
scepticism'.[25]

It is possible that it was not just Fa'apua'a and Fofoa's 'giggly
fibs' that misled Margaret, but preoccupations of her own. One
source of these is to be found in the reading she had done for her
doctorate. While her description of the sexual lives of young
Samoans is unlike that offered by other ethnographers of Samoan
culture, it closely resembles accounts of, for instance, the
Marquesas islanders. Edward Handy had recently claimed of Marquesans that young men and women were totally free sexually:
'every native during the years of adolescence and early maturity
literally ran wild'.[26]

Without necessarily realising that this was what she was doing,
Mead perhaps adopted the notion of a double standard. She may
have assumed that while Samoans remained publicly committed
both to the teachings of the Protestant Church and to their own
rituals of virginity, their sexual behaviour in practice conformed
to the pattern that other anthropologists had attributed to the
Marquesans, and that she took to be characteristic of Polynesia
as a whole.

The likelihood, on the other hand, is that there was a further,
undisclosed source for Mead's claims about the sex lives of
Samoans, and this is to be found in her personal life at the time,
married to Luther Cressman but uncommitted to him. (In her
farewell letter to Luther, she promised, to his understandable dismay, that she would not leave him unless she found someone she
loved more.[27]) It has been suggested that, while on the island of
Tau, she had an affair with a young Samoan. Whether or not this

occurred, it requires only the smallest of interpretative strides to see her beliefs about the sexual liberality of young Samoan girls as a projection of her own liberation. As she was later to say, there were many Americans who then longed to go to the South Seas as an escape 'from a dull and empty routine, from the denial of spontaneity, and the trammelling of individual passions'. When she made clear her destination, she claimed, 'it caused the same breathless stir' as if she were 'setting off for heaven'. People would crowd in on her as if to touch her, while others would hold back 'as from one already set apart for more than earthly delights'.[28]

There is nothing outlandish about young married women having real or imagined affairs when in exotic places; nor about their using the resulting visions of liberality and abundance in shaping the nature and content of their symbolic products. In the literary and visual arts, such erotically charged transformations are an everyday occurrence and are accepted as a matter of course. They become troublesome only when they are offered and accepted as embodying the literal truth. But that is precisely how *Coming of Age in Samoa* was presented and received.

What the Evidence Says

Those who remain loyal to Mead's cause have suggested both that, irrespective of the factual details, *Coming of Age in Samoa* expressed a higher truth – that hers was a 'humane and enlightening vision'; and that her contribution was essentially personal – 'not so much a corpus of knowledge' as the embodiment 'in all her strengths and weaknesses' of what 'it really was to be human and alive'. Another guardian of her reputation has even seemed to suggest that, if judged from a sufficiently up-to-date, post-modern perspective, criticism of Mead's fieldwork in Samoa dissolves away. Where one stands among such representations is to some extent a matter of choice. But there remains, at the heart of the Mead fiasco, an issue which cannot be skirted. It concerns the truth, not as metaphorically conceived or imaginatively transposed, but approached in terms which are starkly matter of fact. Were the sex lives of young Samoans as Mead describes them in *Coming of Age in Samoa* or were they not? If not, and if we are still expected to accept her account as truthful, how are the truths of anthropology to be distinguished from those of the political tract, say, or the theatre?[29]

This question is all the more pressing in a discipline like anthropology where fieldwork is rarely repeated. In the early 1950s, one of Margaret Mead's colleagues, Melville Herskovits, encouraged a research student to do his fieldwork on Mead's island of Tau, with the suggestion that he reappraise her work with 'icy objectivity'.[30] The graduate student chosen, Lowell Holmes, concluded that the reliability of Mead's observations was high, but this did nothing to protect him from her ire. She reprimanded him for failing to clear his restudy with her before he began. When they subsequently met, she accused him of dishonesty; and, later, she gave his book about Tau an unfavourable review.

The simple view is that Mead cheated; and that, both at the time and since, many of her fellow anthropologists have had discreditable reasons for blurring the line over which she stepped – at the lowest, that they had both their departmental grants and their scholarly conceit to defend. But to take this view is seriously to underestimate the temptations that await anthropologists, sociologists or psychologists as they write up their research. For while the human sciences offer the blandishments common to all forms of organised thought, they pose one in an unusually enticing form: that associated with the collective appetite for novelty – for new ways of talking and thinking about human nature and human experience. It is for this reason especially that the Mead fiasco should be seen in its original setting.

The Fiasco in Context

If Margaret Mead was young when she spent her fateful few months in Samoa, so, too, was the discipline of anthropology. As a result, she went into the field, her head ringing with the rhetoric of cultural determinism then being preached by Franz Boas and his disciples, but equipped for fieldwork with little more than a vivid prose style and routine skills acquired while doing an M.A. in psychology and a Ph.D under Boas.[31]

She had, on the other hand, picked up presentational skills. She knew how to dress up her research in order to cover her flanks against attack. That this presentational skill was already part of her armory became apparent once she was in Samoa. With Boas as mentor, she had been funded by the National Research Council specifically to collect evidence about the nature/nurture issue; but she evidently regarded this as a chore. What she really wanted to do was ethnography: to help rescue patterns of living before they were irrevocably lost. As her time in Samoa ran out, Mead became increasingly uneasy about how to satisfy Boas's expectations; and in response to the impending crisis, devised a scheme of research which, while presentationally impeccable, rings hollow. Her claim was that she had a sample of 66 girls, 26 between 8 and 12 years old, 10 between 12 and puberty, and 30 between puberty and about 20 years of age. From these 66 subjects, she said, she would by the end of the next month have the following information: 'Approx. age, rank and birthplace of parent, make-up of household, order of birth, amount of schooling in government school and pastor's school, amount of foreign experience, health and any physical defect, date when puberty was attained, regularity, pain, amount of disability during menstruation; extent to which girl has participated in a knowledge of the current superstitions, taboos, paraphernalia of rank and status; what are her specific ambitions in the way of a choice of husband, number of children, etc.; various domestic industries; her general personality traits, intelligence as measured by observation and by a series of short, well standardized intelligence tests; her friendships, and allegiances within the household, and her general status in her age group'. There would remain 'for special investigation' the sexual lives of her 66 subjects; such issues being 'the most difficult to get at', requiring 'the greatest facility in the language' and the 'longest intimacy'.[32]

Vestiges of this scheme are visible in the appendices to *Coming of Age in Samoa*, but while impressive-looking, it is transparently artefactual. Even if there had been no obstacle of language, such evidence would have taken months rather than weeks to collect; and nowhere does Margaret show that she knew how to move from it to the kinds of information Boas needed – the sort that demanded the greatest facility in the language and the longest intimacy. That Mead should produce so spurious a catalogue for his benefit suggests that she was already adept at putting on a good front; and doing so all the more energetically the weaker her own position threatened to become.

It comes as no surprise to see her abandon the apparatus of data-gathering and resort instead to cross-questioning Fa'apua'a and Fofoa in the course of a trip the three took together in March 1926 to the islands of Ofu and Olosega. It was during this outing that the hoax was perpetrated. Subsequently, in writing up, Mead blurred the relationship between her conclusions and her sources. Without actually saying so, she gives the impression that the picture she paints derives from ethnographical inquiries which were painstaking and dispassionate; whereas in fact, as Derek Freeman has pointed out, the account she gives of the girls' sex lives in the main text of *Coming of Age in Samoa* sits awkwardly with the material in her appendices, and in certain details contradicts it. The fault, again, is as much Boas's as her own. What Mead showed Boas was what he wanted to see; and having seen what he wanted to see, considerations of science and scholarship went by the board.

It would be a mistake, even so, to castigate Mead and Boas in the terms that one might castigate an ambitious and slovenly molecular biologist. In and around the human sciences, as we have said, the appetite for novelty is ravening; and it is those who gratify it who receive the greatest rewards. In the grip of the resulting excitement, human scientists of all complexions can allow their treatment of evidence to become impressionistic, and sometimes – as in Margaret Mead's case – to go haywire.[33] The ensuing confusion is all the more perplexing because – not so much on the strength of evidence as in its interstices – valuable insights may nonetheless accrete.

The Parallel with Freud

While Mead was launching her attack on conventional assumptions about sex and gender, an analogous development was taking place in psychoanalysis, arguably of even deeper significance: the evolution of Freud's 'seduction theory' into his theory of the

Oedipus Complex. Here, too, the relation of theory to documentary evidence collapsed.

The popularly accepted view of this evolution in Freud's thinking is the one that Freud himself promulgated in old age: 'almost all my women patients', he wrote in 1933, 'told me that they had been seduced by their father'.[34] But, he goes on, 'I was driven to recognise in the end that these reports were untrue and so came to understand that hysterical symptoms are derived from fantasies and not from real occurrences'; fantasies which were Oedipal, incestuous. This view is completely at odds, however, with the claims that Freud had himself made nearly four decades earlier in his paper *The Aetiology of Hysteria*, published in 1896.

In that paper, Freud drew on a sample of 18 patients, 12 female and 6 male. The sexual assailants were described as of three types: 'adults who were strangers'; 'a nursery maid or governess or tutor, or, unhappily all too often, a close relative'; and 'children of different sexes, mostly a brother and sister'. In 1896, in other words, there is no explicit mention of fathers; and the problems of father/daughter incest are not posed. Furthermore, it was Freud's contention at the time that his patients suffered hysterical symptoms precisely because all memory of their molestation had been repressed. What his patients produced were fantasies, associations and dreams which Freud *interpreted* as reflecting actual sexual molestation.

In 1905, Freud distanced himself from his earlier claim that the seductions were real seductions; and in 1914 made it plain that the idea was a dangerous mistake: one 'which might have been almost fatal to the young science' of psychoanalysis. But it is only much later, in his *Autobiographical Study* of 1925, that he for the first time implicates fathers as 'almost always' the guilty parties. If he had known all along that fathers were guilty – whether in fact or in their daughters' fantasies – why did he not say so earlier; in 1896 or, at the latest, in 1905?

In a much discussed letter to Wilhelm Fliess, written in 1897, Freud seems both to identify fathers as molesters, *and* to abandon his seduction theory as implausible. He says 'that in all cases, the father, not excluding my own, had to be accused of being perverse'. Such an imputation, he assumes, is far-fetched. He also makes it clear that he has decided to say nothing about his mistake: 'I shall not tell it in Dan, nor speak of it in Askelon, in the

land of the Philistines.'[35] This new insight of Freud's is flatly
incompatible with the factual descriptions of assailants he had
offered in print only a year before.[36]

Why, having suppressed his change of mind for nearly thirty
years, did Freud at last speak out about it in 1925? A plausible explanation is that he was moved to do so by a significant
development in his personal life. A few years earlier, contrary both
to good sense and to the implications of his own theory, he had
begun to psychoanalyse his own daughter Anna. This analysis
lasted four years, and took place when Anna, the youngest of his
six children, was in her mid-twenties.[37] She was to remain
unmarried, and became fiercely protective of her father's memory.
Granted the deep and thorough analysis of his daughter he
claimed to have undertaken, it follows that Freud must have confronted not only her incestuous wishes towards him, but his
towards her. (Viewed narrowly, Freud was using his role as a
clinician to legitimate his access to his favourite daughter. That
the traffic between them in erotic thoughts and needs was formal-
ised and non-reciprocal does not detract in the least from the
impropriety of what he was doing.)

What Went Wrong?

As she drafted *Coming of Age in Samoa*, Mead followed the otherwise inexplicable path she did, this parallel suggests, because she
was in the grip of a luminous insight. The stories she had been
told by Fa'apua'a and Fofoa resonated with what she had learnt
from fellow anthropologists like Edward Handy about the sexual
licence of Polynesian adolescents; and both resonated with the liberation she experienced in shaking herself clear of her stodgy
upbringing and her 'student marriage' to Cressman. There may
also have been more literary echoes: Herman Melville's talk in
Typee of 'naked houries' and of 'wilful, care-killing damsels'. At
the back of Mead's mind there could have lurked the conviction,
strong in white, middle-class American homes, that young black
women are sexually free. At some point, the confluence of these
disparate perceptions and fantasies will have become overwhelming, filling her mind with a truth that had to be told. By the time

her report for the National Research Council had Boas's approval, and she came to convert it into a text acceptable to her publisher William Morrow, she seems to have been committed neck and crop to the vision of the Samoans' unbridled sexual liberality.

Melville Herskovits would tease Mead, Cressman claimed, about her attitude towards evidence. If evidence proved recalcitrant, Herskovits insisted, she would react by saying 'If it isn't, it ought to be.' And, then, if challenged, she would justify herself by asking 'Well, what's so bad about that?'[38] Perhaps the most economical explanation of the Mead debacle is that when imaginatively seized she became genuinely insensitive to the contract implicit in the factual claims she made. For her a story was true if it carried an unusually powerful persuasive charge; if it enabled her to execute a psychological manoeuvre she needed to execute; and if it placed a listening audience in the palm of her hand.

In as much as she could grasp the distinction between facts and wishes, she will have seen it as bearing on others, not herself; and certainly not on herself when in a state of high drive. At such times, she was eloquent in the service of a vision, and evidence became ammunition.[39]

When, in 1964, Margaret Mead learnt from Derek Freeman that the fieldwork others had done in Samoa had shown her to be mistaken, she was, he says, visibly shaken. But she did not alter her text. In her last preface to *Coming of Age in Samoa*, written in 1972, she says 'It must remain, as all anthropological works must remain, exactly as it was written, true to what I saw in Samoa and what I was able to convey of what I saw ...' [40] Where Freud plainly understood that his initial reading of his evidence had placed him in a tight corner, and that dissimulation was required if he was not to lose face, Mead's attitude seems, to the end, to have been more blithe. Neither to her audience, nor even perhaps to herself, did she adequately acknowledge that Samoan culture in the mid-1920s was a slice of the natural order, and that her account of it was in some ascertainable degree either accurate or flawed.[41]

CHAPTER FOUR

At Close Quarters

IF OUR THOUGHT EXPERIMENT has succeeded as we hope, and if the needs and perceptions of the two sexes differ from one another in the subtle ways we believe they do, it is easy to see how love affairs and marriages turn into battlegrounds. Of the four women whose lives we have described, three paid critical attention to the conventions of marriage and family life. Millett's posture was insurrectionary. More moderate, Mead never tired of expatiating on the virtues of the extended family and the vices of the nuclear one; and Brittain, too, wrote about marriage. In the guise of Professor Minerva Huxterwin – a laboured amalgamation of Huxley and Darwin – she predicted in *Halcyon* that monogamy would endure, but only because 'No other relationship appears so well fitted to leave the mind free from the fret of sexual urge by adequately satisfying the demands of the body without giving to them that degree of attention which renders sex an incubus rather than an inspiration to mankind.'[1] In keeping with this prophylactic view, she envisaged 'second contracts' for husbands living apart from their wives.

In the last twenty years, the mood of disenchantment has become more pervasive, and has expressed itself in a burgeoning literature of complaint. In this, marriage is seen as hostile to the needs of both parties, especially those of women; and as an arrangement that, if it cannot be re-engineered, must be overthrown.

Our next step is to articulate these discontents, being as clear as we can about what is changing and what is not. First, however, we examine a phenomenon, rare in statistical terms, but influential at the level of expectation and fantasy: that of highly educated and liberally nurtured young women who become revolutionaries, not on the page like Kate Millett, nor in the mind's eye, but in violent practice.

Fighting it Out on the Platz

Women terrorists are important to our argument because they embody an alternative that still carries with it a distinctive *frisson* of excitement, and that, simply by existing, opens doors on to hitherto unformulated ways of being a woman. Gudrun Ensslin's story is as eloquent in this respect as any. A moving spirit of Germany's Red Army Faction, she and her lover Andreas Baader were imprisoned in 1977; and on the same day, six months later, both committed suicide.[2]

Gudrun was born in 1940, her father a pastor in the Evangelical Church in Germany, who claimed to be a descendant of the philosopher Hegel. She helped her mother, worked hard at school, played the violin, taught Bible classes, and sang the Lutheran hymns 'At All Times Sing Hallelujah!', 'Is Your Life Full of Guilt?', and 'Must I Then, Must I Then from the Little Town Depart?' She grew up learning to favour the reunification of Germany and nuclear disarmament, to dwell on the sufferings of the Third World, and to feel contempt for materialistic greed. When eighteen, she spent a year in Pennsylvania under the auspices of the International Christian Youth Exchange.

On her return from America, Gudrun went to the University of Tübingen to study philosophy. There she met a young man named Bernward Vesper, whose father had been a poet of the 'Blood and Soil' school favoured by the Nazis ('My Fuhrer, at every hour,' he had written, 'Germany, Germany, knows what a weight/You bear, and how at your heart's core/You fight and win the burdensome battle of fate.') Gudrun and Bernward travelled to Spain together and hid in the Alhambra over night to consummate their love. In those days, according to Vesper's half-sister, Gudrun was 'so quiet, she seemed to hang on his lips, you didn't even know she had an opinion of her own until you got her alone without him.'[3] They read Marx, Marcuse and Mao, and together they published a pacifist anthology *Against Death – Voices Against the Atom Bomb*. The couple became engaged and moved to Berlin, where she joined the Free University and started a doctorate on the poet Hans Henny Jahn. In Berlin, they both worked hard for the Social Democrats, became disillusioned, and moved, as many were then moving, into the politics of street protest.

It was at this point that Gudrun began to detach herself from the values of her Lutheran upbringing. She and Vesper had a son, Felix, but before his birth, the couple became estranged. She took a leading role in what Jillian Becker describes as 'a short porno film',[4] came into conflict with the police for distributing leaflets defamatory of the Berlin state prosecutor, and used pepper to disrupt a concert given by Pierre Boulez. The state was 'fascist', she now believed; and instead of demonstrating turbulently but peacefully, she was determined to 'fight it out on the Platz'.

'White-faced, intense, shrill-voiced', Ensslin then fell in love with Baader; and, abandoning her son Felix, went to live with him. Baader taught her how to steal fast cars; and she, in response, found him closer to reality than anyone she had known. Theirs has been described as a 'marriage of fanaticism and unscrupulousness'; Baader bringing to it 'the will to commit crime', Ensslin 'the grand pretext for doing so'.[5] Hers was 'the kind of fervour which old religious wars, crusades, and persecutions had been fired with'.[6] Gunter Grass who knew her in Berlin, described her as 'idealistic, with an inbuilt loathing for any compromise'. She had 'a yearning', he said, 'for the Absolute, the perfect solution'.[7] The court psychiatrist said of her that she was 'capable of hating in a very elementary fashion'. She was in his view the backbone of the Red Army Faction, 'arrogant, ruthless, and coercive'.[8] Once individuals or groups had been tarred with ideological guilt, she felt free to act towards them with a viciousness one would otherwise regard as psychopathic. Within our own developmental model, she stands as the embodiment of a distinctively 'female' characteristic: the tendency of women to structure their imaginative resources in terms of responsibility and blame.

A feature of the revolutionary method adopted by Ensslin and her colleagues was a formidable brutality of utterance. Three days after Baader had been sprung from prison in 1970, their press release read as follows: 'Did the pigs really believe that we would let Comrade Baader sit in jail for two or three years? Did any pig really believe we would talk about the development of class struggle, the reorganization of the proletariat, without arming ourselves at the same time? Did the pigs who shot first believe that we would allow ourselves without violence to be shot off like slaughter-cattle? Whoever does not defend himself will die. Start the armed resistance! Build up the Red Army!'[9] When eventually brought to trial, Ensslin and Baader roundly abused the court.

Baader yelled at the judge that he was an 'arse-hole', while Ensslin shrieked at him that, yes, they were going to disturb his court's proceedings, and she denounced, too, the state-appointed defenders, screaming that 'If those pigs over there open their snouts once more, we will go. Either them or us!'[10] Notwithstanding this barrage of abuse, they were tried – largely it seems in their absence – and, nearly two years later, found guilty of four murders, thirty-four attempted murders, six bombings and a variety of other crimes including criminal conspiracy. Each was sentenced to three times life, plus fifteen years. In passing sentence, the judges itemised the people whom the gang had made into scapegoats for 'American imperialism': not only soldiers, but printers, proof-readers, housewives, a tourist group, a child riding a scooter on the pavement. They also quoted back to the accused a phrase used by Ensslin in the book she had edited with Vesper: 'Everyone has a right to die a natural death.'[11]

It would be a mistake, nevertheless, to see all women terrorists following a single path. Like Ensslin, Ulrike Meinhof had been devoutly religious as a student, and had been active in the politics of the moderate left. But she had then joined the ranks of the Gucci radicals or *Schili*; and, as a journalist and television personality, became a household name. Even with the benefit of hindsight, there is nothing about her life as a young married woman to indicate the abrupt stride she would take towards extremism. Photographs show her smiling back at the lens as many young German matrons were then smiling, assured of lavish material benefits in store. It was only when her marriage to a fellow journalist foundered that this stride was taken. In the course of a few months, she joined the Red Army Faction, abandoning her seven-year-old twin daughters to do so. (Ensslin, who viewed Meinhof with contempt, packed the twins off to a training camp for terrorists in the Middle East; a fate from which they were rescued by their father only at the last minute.) Later, Meinhof was arrested; and, like Baader and Ensslin, committed suicide in prison.

Susanna Ronconi, founder and joint leader of the Italian Prime Linea, presents a pattern at once analogous but different again. While both Ensslin and Meinhof can be seen as rejecting the feminine – and more specifically maternal – side of their natures to become outlaws, Ronconi had an intimate and enduring relationship with her mother, apparently a civilised and moderate figure, and saw her own ability to kill as part of her femininity.[12]

Ronconi grew up, she was later to claim, a happy and dreamy child spending hours alone listening to music with her dog lying beside her. She rebelled in her teens, became active in Italian student politics, and later joined the Red Brigades. However, like Ulrike Meinhof – and like Margaret Mead – she craved a 'family'. Finding the secrecy and lack of companionship of the Red Brigades intolerable, she created a family of her own, Prime Linea. Ronconi organised and took part in assassinations, bank raids, knee-cappings; and the viciousness of these operations is beyond question. A widely respected and liberal-minded judge, Emilio Alessandrini, was assassinated because he was suspected of investigating not only neo-Fascist groups but Prime Linea. On another occasion, Prime Linea, led by Ronconi, raided the Turin School of Industrial Management, took nearly two hundred students and lecturers hostage, and knee-capped five of each, as a warning to all 'oppressors of the people'. Such killing and wounding Ronconi later described as 'an atrocious experience, each one very different'. While some of the young men had 'a mania for guns' and treated them as fetishes, for the women this was never so. Their commitment was deeper. The dominant emotion was one of fear; the dominant sense, one of 'crossing a threshold'. But such violence was linked in turn, she believed, to maternity: 'It is the woman who gives life; it is the woman who also takes life.'[13]

Incarcerated for a second time, now for thirty years, Ronconi dissociated herself from her revolutionary past, thus earning herself a shorter sentence, daily meetings with her fellow revolutionary Sergio Segio (previously her lover and now her husband), regular work outside the prison, and forty-five days holiday a year. Her most bitter regret is that, while on the run, she had not found it possible to visit her mother who was dying of cancer. Especially precious is the recollection of her escape from prison, before her eventual re-arrest. Segio planned and executed the breakout. 'I was very moved, because he had left Prime Linea, but he came back for me.' 'It was', she says, 'one of the best moments of my life.'[14]

For Ensslin and Ronconi, particularly, it was not a question of renouncing love for politics, but of recasting love and intimacy within a context that seemed morally sound. If the memory of their insurrection lingers, so too do its confusions, not least those about the role of revolutionary theory in directing and legitimating revolutionary action. It was an issue on which the philosophers of the time were to reveal themselves notably equivocal. Herbert Marcuse had first published *Eros and Civilization* in 1955, and the political preface he wrote for it in 1966 ends with the battle cry: 'Today the fight for life, the fight for Eros, is the *political* fight.'[15] But, as the students of Berlin's Free University were to discover when he addressed them the following year and again in 1968, his instinct was to draw back from revolution's brink. His wife, on the other hand, was more forthright. She carried off Hannah Tillich, the long-suffering wife of the theologian, to a peace demonstration, during which Joan Baez sang and eggs were thrown at Erich Fromm. Subsequently, Hannah recalls, 'the Marcuses came to dinner at our house after Kennedy's election and we women had a sharp argument about loyalty to the United States, which had taken us in as émigrés and from which we had received every advantage and help. She was now glorying in tearing down the influence of that government. The two men sat by while we raved.'[16]

Sometimes the philosophers lapsed into absurdity. Conspicuously credulous were the comments Jean-Paul Sartre made to the press, having travelled to visit Andreas Baader on hunger strike in prison.[17] More purely comic, but perhaps apocryphal, was Theodor Adorno's response to the women who attended his lectures and bared their breasts as an expression of the 'praxis' (or practice) his teaching was seen to advocate. Mortified, Adorno disavowed action of any sort. 'I am', he averred, 'a theoretical person.'[18] Jürgen Habermas likewise seemed to endorse revolution in principle but withdrew from it in the event, distinguishing finely, perhaps opportunistically, between demonstrational force, of which he approved, and the provocation of declared and manifest violence, of which he did not.[19]

The question of whether revolutionary 'praxis' is a purely cerebral matter, or is in Ensslin's terms a question of 'fighting it out on the Platz', the theorists of the Frankfurt School left unresolved. As we shall see, an analogous air of uncertainty hangs over the works of the next generation of radical philosophers, notably Michel Foucault and Jacques Derrida. It remains unclear whether they are to be read literally or with tongue in cheek.

The Literature of Complaint

Relatively few young women from similar homes have strayed across the line that Ensslin, Meinhof and Ronconi crossed; but any number are now free to imagine their personal lives subject to equally radical revision. Each year, the literature of complaint about marriage grows more abundant. An appreciable proportion of such writing rejects men or belittles them, while a further proportion remains committed to thoughts of heterosexual intimacy and love but expresses the wish that men were other than they are.

The mood is well caught in Shere Hite's *Women and Love*, a compilation no less disquieting for resting, evidentially speaking, on so very insecure a foundation.[20] Hite's method is to distribute open-ended questionnaires in an unregulated way, and to analyse the responses of those who reply, subjecting them in doing so to massive and undisclosed editorial attention. Of 100,000 distributed in the present instance, she claims, 4,500 were returned to her. Not only is her sample self-selecting, in other words; the responses given may well have been influenced by her respondents' perception of her as a famous feminist, exceptionally outspoken in sexual matters; by the thought of replying to her personally; and by the opportunity to do so anonymously. While offered as fact, her evidence has the status of polemic-with-numbers.

These are among the views which, Hite says, her respondents overwhelmingly share: 98% would like their husband or lover to talk more about his feelings, thoughts, and dreams, and ask them more about their own; 96% believe that they are giving more emotional support than they are getting; 95% report forms of emotional and psychological harassment from men with whom they are intimate; 95% see men as assuming that they will take first place psychologically in a relationship; 94% describe very close, important, and enjoyable friendships with other women; 93% believe they are trying harder to make their relationships work than are men; 91% initiate divorce when this occurs; 89% feel torn between men's demands for love, their duty to be giving and supportive of others, and their need to have time for their own thoughts and ideas; 89% of women who are separated or divorced say that they were lonelier in marriage than at any other time in their lives; 89% emphasise that they want to make their relationships with men as close, happy, and equal as their relationships with their women friends; 88% say the men in their lives prefer to avoid talking things over, and that insistence can lead to an argument; 88% say they want more equal emotional relationships with the men they love; 87% find it difficult to meet men they admire and respect; 87% say they feel they are not really 'seen' by the men they are with; 87% say they think men are more emotionally dependent on women than women on men after the first few months of a relationship or marriage; 87% have had, at one time or another, relationships that were painful or draining; 87% say that their relationships with other women are emotionally closer than their love relationships with men; 85% say the most wonderful quality of their friendships with women is the ability to talk freely and openly without being judged, to be truly listened to.[21]

If Hite's evidence is murky, the burden of her presentation is crystal clear. The ideal of romantic, heterosexual love, while alive in the mind of her respondents, is failing to deliver its supposed benefits. The institution of marriage is on the verge of collapse, and alternative forms of intimacy should urgently be sought.

This disillusion now permeates the kinds of journalism explicitly directed to young unmarried women. *Ms London* is preeminently the kind of material read and abandoned on the London Underground. A vehicle for advertisements and distributed free, it also contains feature articles. In a recent edition, the lead article, accompanied by a photograph showing its author to be youthful, feminine and well-groomed, concerned chastity. 'A recent survey revealed', she claims, 'that more women in this country would prefer to abstain from sexual activity than from chocolate. I understand that. For one thing, a bar of chocolate usually lasts longer. It is also unlikely to stay snoring flatulently in your bed until lunchtime.'[22] Sex remains culturally obligatory; it is 'Michael Douglas and Sharon Stone, soft-focus and carefully-planned camera angles, body-doubles and retakes'. But passion is hard to sustain in the face of reality – whether in the form of the 'poorly-evolved ape descendant' male companion, or of recent demonstrations of the female orgasm on television, and the knowledge 'that your moment of ecstasy looks disconcertingly like someone wringing out a soggy pink swimsuit'.

The tone of such writing is tough-minded, and its derogatory

jokes imply a jockeying for power with men, not only in the work-
place but in bed. Sex, its author suggests, easily becomes 'less
about the earth moving and more about a little sod shifting under-
neath you'.

Divorce

While internally consistent and powerfully persuasive, the vision
promoted by such popular writing, whether Hite's or *Ms
London*'s, is nonetheless at odds with the view of intimate life
which emerges from factual research.

The divorce statistics for England and Wales, it is true, show
that in 1991 there were just over half as many divorces as marriages; that this proportion had risen appreciably since 1981 (51%
as opposed to 41%); and that during the decade 1982–91, the
parents of a million and a half children under the age of 16 had
divorced.[23]

But if rates of divorce have increased, they have done so in complex ways, being by no means uniform, for instance, between
countries that are immediate neighbours. In the 1930s, French
marriages were seven times as likely to end in divorce as ones in
England and Wales. From that point onwards, the percentage of
divorces per 100 marriages increased steadily in France, whereas in
England and Wales, after the war especially, it increased by leaps
and bounds. In 1935 the French rate stood at 7%; that in England
and Wales at 1%. By 1981, the equivalent figures were 24% and
39%. In 1935, the percentage of divorces per 100 marriages in
Sweden was the same as in France; but, like the English rate, it
too rose sharply, reaching a peak of 52% in 1977, dropping back
to 44% in 1981 and then beginning to climb again, but this time
more slowly.[24]

The most recent data for England and Wales are in any case
by no means entirely gloomy. You find that while the number of
middle-aged people divorcing is still going up, the number of
those under twenty-five is dropping, among young women especially (where 19,812 young women aged between twenty and
twenty-four divorced in 1981, only 14,639 did so in 1991). As
striking is the evidence about the age at marriage of couples who

subsequently divorce. The number of those who divorce having married one another when they were in their late twenties or early thirties continues to climb; but, meanwhile, the number divorcing who married as teenagers is dropping. At present, the position in England and Wales is that the number of divorces is still rising among the middle aged, among those who have been married for a substantial period of time rather than relatively briefly, and among those who have already been divorced at least once. For the rest, the impression is of divorce rates which in historical terms are very high, but which, for the last decade, have been relatively stable.

It may nonetheless be true that, over the last half century or so, the balance of pleasure and pain in married life has changed little. Rather than there being a late twentieth-century descent from order into chaos, there may always have been a sizeable proportion of married couples who got on wretchedly together, but who previously lacked the financial resources or legal opportunity to divorce. Equally, there may always have been a large proportion, perhaps the majority, who jogged along tolerably well together, enduring the occasional crisis or disillusionment; and a further proportion – perhaps as large as a quarter of the total, even a third – who were mutually devoted.[25]

Adultery

The statistical evidence and texts like Hite's again part company over the question of adultery. While 83% of Hite's respondents believe in monogamy as an ideal way of life, 70% of those who have been married for five years or more claim to be having sex outside marriage. Of these, 89% keep their affairs secret, 76% say that their main reason for being unfaithful is alienation from their husbands, and 76% experience no guilt. Guilt-free adultery, these 'data' suggest, is the norm.[26]

However, the authors of a recent survey of 18,876 British people between the ages of sixteen and fifty-nine make it clear that 'concurrent' sexual relationships are very much the exception.[27] The vast majority of married men and women report themselves as having been monogamous for the last five years. Fewer than 1 in

20 married men and fewer than 1 in 50 married women report having had more than one sexual partner in that period; and even fewer – about 1 in a 100 married men and 1 in 500 married women – report more than two.[28] Even among the single and uncommitted, the dominant pattern is that of 'serial' relationships rather than concurrent ones. The only oddity of these findings concerns 'cohabitation'; the stable heterosexual relationship outside marriage. Cohabiting men are more rather than less likely than single ones to report relationships which are concurrent.

In terms of attitude, the weight of opinion revealed by this survey is conspicuously indulgent towards premarital sex; conspicuously censorious towards sex which is extramarital. Only 8% of the men and 11% of the women interviewed believe that premarital sex is always or mostly wrong; whereas 79% of the men and 84% of the women see extramarital sex as always or mostly wrong. Even among those who are cohabiting rather than married, two-thirds of men and three-quarters of women believe that such relationships should be sexually exclusive.[29] This faith in monogamy is at least as strong among the younger members of the sample as the older. There is also support for the view that monogamy is the most pleasurable pattern. More than two-thirds of the sample agree that 'sex tends to get better the longer you know someone'; and only a fifth disagree with the claim that 'a person who sticks with one partner is likely to have a more satisfying sex life than someone who has many partners'.

The Influence of Intelligence

The literature of complaint parts company with the factual evidence for a third time over the question of intelligence. In earlier generations it was taken for granted that it was the simple girl who 'fell'; the intelligent and well-born who, despite the occasional lapse, became pregnant when it suited their interests to do so: that is to say, within wedlock. It is this pattern that the sexual revolution is thought to have changed out of recognition, modern women now having children out of wedlock as a matter of course because they judge it appropriate to do so.

Recent survey evidence tells a different story. The most persuasive comes from the follow-up, across the decade from 1980 to 1990, of young American men and women taking part in the National Longitudinal Survey of Youth. Of the white women in this sample who went to college and gained a degree, a high proportion have had children. Of those children, 99% were born in wedlock. The equivalent figure among those white women who finished their education at the level of the high school diploma is 87%; appreciably lower, but still high. In terms of measured intelligence, this second group is broad, containing some women with relatively high IQs and some whose IQs are relatively low. Within it, less than 3% of those with IQs of 130 or higher had their first child out of wedlock, whereas 34% of those with IQs of 70 or lower did so.[30]

More generally, the evidence from this survey shows that the rates of birth outside marriage drop quite sharply the higher the mothers' measured intelligence; and that this is so largely irrespective of their socio-economic status. In contrast to young white women categorised in terms of IQ as very dull, those categorised as very bright will marry later, on average by four years; be half as likely to divorce within the first five years of marriage; and be fifteen times less likely to give birth to an illegitimate baby.

As matters now stand, this evidence suggests, a fifth of American children are now being born to unmarried mothers whose IQs are well below average. These children are more likely than others to be underweight at birth, and live in squalid conditions. When they grow up, they will tend to have low IQs, to fare poorly in the job market, to have social and behavioural problems, and to spend time in prison. They will be less likely than their contemporaries to marry; more likely to have children out of wedlock.[31] It is not a comforting picture.

What is Changing and Why?

Arguably, the dilemmas of the underclass in the modern state are those of the poor and underprivileged everywhere, although intensified, now, by the visions of boundless opportunity they see whenever they turn on a television set. Among the privileged, on the other hand, change has been vertiginous. The circumstances now surrounding prosperous adolescents and young adults bear little resemblance to those that surrounded Vera Brittain, Margaret Thatcher or Margaret Mead – or, for that matter, Gudrun Ensslin, Ulrike Meinhof or Susanna Ronconi. Where, as recently as forty years ago, many intelligent and resourceful young women were ignorant about sex and were intent on marrying as virgins, they now see themselves as entitled to sexual experience, and as subject in this respect only to those constraints they judge appropriate. The age at which sexual intercourse first occurs has dropped markedly: for women born between 1931 and 1935, the median age at first intercourse was twenty-one, whereas for those born between 1966 and 1975, the median is seventeen, the fall being nearly as marked among men.[32] Among the younger cohorts in the British survey, the marriage of virgins is as a result quite rare.

The pattern of female virginity followed by life-long marriage is now seriously challenged by that of serial monogamy; indeed, there is increasingly the possibility that the second pattern could supplant the first. This transformation is widely seen as a consequence of a pharmacological invention: the contraceptive pill. It is assumed that this invention, releasing young women from the risk of pregnancy, empowered them to explore their own desires in just the way that young men do. While attractively simple, this belief, like others, falls foul of recent evidence. The British survey data show that the sharpest drop in the age at which young women first have intercourse took place in the 1950s, whereas the contraceptive pill was not prescribed until 1961, and was in practice unavailable to unmarried women until 1972.[33]

Whatever such changes in sexual behaviour indicate, the difficulties intrinsic to the heterosexual relationship remain unexamined. These afflict rich and poor, liberated and more backward-looking alike; and it is these we want to make explicit next.

CHAPTER FIVE

The Hidden Algebra

THE DIFFICULTIES INHERENT IN close relations between the sexes organise themselves around a restricted set of themes. Often unacknowledged, and in certain climates unacknowledge-able, these themes constitute a species of psychic 'algebra', hidden beneath the surface of love affairs and marriages. Here we deal with two: the management of the past, and the dilemmas of deception and disclosure. Both can give rise to uncontrollable jealousy and the sense of irreparable loss.

In the first half of this chapter, we illustrate these themes. Rather than separating them out, we leave them, as they are in life, interwoven; and we turn to fiction because it frees authors to tell the truth with especial accuracy and candour. In the second half, we follow the trail of those theorists who, in the course of the last thirty years or so, have attempted to make sense of the anxiety and alienation that excitement so often brings in its wake.

Graham and Ann

The novelist Julian Barnes has noted that husbands may not only be haunted by their wives's pasts, but be morbidly curious about them. The hero of his *Before She Met Me*, Graham Hendrick, is a historian in his early forties who leaves his wife Barbara for another woman, Ann.[1] Barbara had approached married life as if it were trench warfare. One of her devices, Graham recalls, was to pile the bedclothes on top of him while he slept, then wake him and berate him for stealing them; her aim to instill a sense of guilt. Another of his exchanges with Barbara he remembers with parti-cular clarity. 'One evening in the seventh year of their marriage, after a dinner almost without tension', he had felt 'as soothed and

happy as had seemed then to be possible. . . . He had said to Barbara, exaggerating only a little, "I feel very happy." And Barbara,
who was scouring the final crumbs from the dinner-table, had
wheeled round, pink rubber gloves wetly aloft, as if she were
a poised surgeon, and answered, "What are you trying to get
out of?"[2]

Ann frees him from the attrition of domestic cut-and-thrust,
and stirs in him a sense of life's abundance. In matters of sex, she
offers the distinctively modern virtue of candour: 'never coy, or
sly, or evasive'.[3] He intuits 'not so much that Ann represented his
last chance, but that she had always represented his first and only
chance'.[4] 'One thought recurred like a bass figure in his new life,
and brought him a strange comfort. At least now, he would say to
himself, now that I've got Ann, at least now I'll be properly
mourned.'[5]

But in falling in love with Ann and marrying her, Graham spills
across the boundary which separates them as beings. He lists in his
diary what she is wearing each day as she goes to work, and sur-
reptitiously consults this list while conducting tutorials. He clears
the table after supper, and eats what she has left on her plate.
Once this existential boundary has been breached, he finds himself
haunted by thoughts of the men in her past: the Bennys and
Chrises and Lymans and Phils and Jeds. As Freud would have predicted, his curiosity turns into 'research', and this becomes
obsessive. Seeking out the humdrum films in which Ann has
played small parts, he falls into ungovernable ruminations about
whether she slept in the flesh with the actors she pretended to
sleep with on celluloid. By gaining physical access to Ann, these
men have unwittingly gained access to Graham's head. His
jealousy 'came in rushes, in sudden, intimate bursts' that winded
him.[6] They also left him in the grip of a necessity: to know what
Ann had or had not done with each of the men in question.

If women like Ann can be candid and commonsensical, it is increasingly argued, men like Graham should be candid and
commonsensical in return. Both should be *mature*. But, Barnes's
tale implies, love affairs and marriages are not venues for the
deployment of maturity or commonsense. If they were, lovers
would be colleagues, and the passion that intimacy now harnesses
would either become blunted or move elsewhere. Among the
remedies offered to Graham by his worldly-wise friend Jack is that

he should 'love her less'. 'You don't have to hate her or dislike her or anything . . . Just learn to detach yourself a little . . .' [7] But the ghastly Jack, too, has had an affair with Ann. A mood of slaughterhouse brutality supervenes, and the narrative ends with Graham killing both Jack and himself.

Barnes describes forcefully what sociologists like Lillian Rubin are discovering in interviews.[8] A wife can find that her husband hates her, apparently arbitrarily, for things she did before she knew of his existence. Reasonably, young women expect the same sexual freedom as young men; and many young men either willingly endorse this facet of sexual equality, or – finding that they can articulate no socially acceptable alternative – pay it lip-service. But perplexing choices ensue. The wife may elect to tell her husband the truth about her past, hoping, often mistakenly, that this will establish between them a climate of mutual trust. Alternatively, she may pretend that she does not have a past: that what occurred did not occur; or, if it did, that it lacked meaning.

Attempting to turn the tide, the philosopher Roger Scruton has used the destructive capacity of sexual jealousy as the basis for an argument in favour of the institution of marriage and of a policy of faithfulness within it. 'Because jealousy is one of the greatest of psychical catastrophes, involving the possible ruin of both partners, a morality based in the need for erotic love must forestall and eliminate jealousy. It is in the deepest human interest, therefore, that we form the habit of fidelity. This habit is natural and normal; but it is also easily broken, and the temptation to break it is contained in desire itself – in the element of generality which tempts us always to experiment, to verify, to detach ourselves from what is too familiar in the interest of excitement and risk.'[9]

Unfortunately, recommendations like Scruton's overestimate the extent to which desire and its consequences are under conscious control. As authors like Doris Lessing show, desire is imperative; inseparable from the prospect of life before death.

Muriel and Henry, Althea and Frederick

Among Lessing's stories, there is one, published in the early 1970s, that attempts to schematise modern marriage.[10] A species of working example, there is a sense in which it could have been written by a psychologist. At one level, it is a story of matrimonial double-dealing; more obliquely, it is about the failure of seemingly enlightened values to shape and accommodate the characters' compelling needs.

Lessing describes two couples, the Smiths and Joneses; a tight-knit foursome. The husbands are doctors who, in a mood of post-war optimism and high-mindedness, decide to set up a joint practice. The two unions, 'both as happy as marriages are, both exemplary from society's point of view', nonetheless contained 'a shocking flaw, a secret cancer, a hidden vice'.[11]

The couples meet for the first time over a meal to celebrate the launch of the new practice. On their way home, Frederick Jones and Muriel Smith, without premeditation or subsequent guilt, have sexual intercourse in a wood, 'with vigour and relish and enjoyment'. This pattern endures: 'having separated, they did not think about what had happened, nor consider their partners: it was as if these occasions belonged to another plane altogether – that trivial, sordid, and unimportant, that friendly, goodnatured and entirely enjoyable plane that lay beside, or above, or within these two so satisfactory marriages'.[12]

It is not just Frederick and Muriel's actions which complicate the pattern. Later Althea Jones, the innocent wife, falls in love with a younger doctor, goes furtively to bed with him, confides in Muriel, and suffers deeply. Later still, Frederick, the guilty husband, falls head over heels in love with the practice's young receptionist, Frances. He in turn suffers, threatens divorce and suicide, and claims never to have experienced real love before.

The repercussions of Frederick's new passion overwhelm Muriel. She now suffers too, 'submerged under waves of jealousy of the young girl'. Her husband Henry 'she had always known, was a cold fish. Their happiness had been a half-thing. Her own potential had always been in cold storage. And so she raged and suffered, for the sake of Frederick, her real love . . .' That was what Muriel felt. 'What she *thought*, and knew, was that she was mad. Everything she now felt had nothing, but nothing to do with her long relationship with Frederick, which was as pleasant as a good healthy diet and as unremarkable, and nothing to do with her marriage with Henry, whom she loved deeply, and who made her happy, and whose humorous and civilised company she enjoyed more than anyone's.'[13]

The receptionist departs, Henry dies, and Frederick, Althea and Muriel live together as a single household. The two women are one another's intimates, but it does not cross Althea's mind (and never will) that her husband is sleeping with them both. 'Often, when the three of them were together, Althea would look at those two, her husband, her closest friend, and think: Of course, if I died, they would marry.' Her old friend 'was a well into which confidences vanished and were forgotten; Muriel never gossiped, never condemned. She was the soul – if one could use that old-fashioned word – of honour. As for Frederick, when he had fallen in love, not only his wife, but the whole world had known of it: he was not a man who could, or who wanted to, conceal his feelings. But the real thing was this: the three of them had made, and now lived inside, an edifice of kindliness and responsibility and decency; it was simply not possible that it could harbour deception.'[14]

One night, as the household waits for Frederick to return, Althea realises that her own future and Muriel's are tied together. The likelihood is that they will survive Frederick and live on together alone. It is not a pleasurable prospect; more a premonition. And there Lessing leaves them; and leaves us, each in our own way discomforted.

Viewing the Smiths and Joneses with the benefit of the distance Lessing's manner provides, there is the sense of the four actors – and, by implication, ourselves – not as puppets exactly, but as the creatures of an engine at work behind the scenery. They do not know it is there, let alone how to intervene in its workings; yet, paradoxically, it is nowhere if not within them. They exist in a strange state with regard to the truth about themselves, somewhere between sleepwalking, self-deception and false consciousness.

What interests Lessing are the contortions of intimate need that Frederick, Muriel and Althea experience; miseries that neither candour nor prudence would necessarily have short-circuited. Years after Frederick fell in love with Frances, she returns to haunt him. 'His intelligence told him everything it ought, such as that if he had been fool enough to leave Althea for Frances, or if Frances had been fool enough to marry him, in a very short time Frances would have been a dear known face on a shared pillow, and what Frances had represented would have moved its quarters elsewhere.'[15] He realises that Frances, 'a lovely but quite ordinary girl, must be a stand-in for something else. It must be so. No small human being could possibly support the weight of such a force and a fierceness of longing, of want, of need'. But she haunts him nonetheless. 'His life was divided between dark, or perhaps a clear flat grey, and light – Frances. Between everything heavy, plodding, difficult, and everything delicious – Frances. Nothing in his actual life fed delight or sprang from it; somewhere else was a sweetness and ease which he had known once, when he had loved Frances.'[16]

As they age, Althea looks back, and she too divides what she sees into light and dark. 'For her, the sunlit time lay on the other side of the affair with the young doctor. It was not the physical thing she regretted, no; it was that she had not told her husband. Time had done nothing at all to soften her guilt about it. Frederick and she had known a time of perfection, of complete trust and belief. Then she, Althea, had chosen to destroy it.'[17] He had fallen so violently in love with Frances because 'she had told him lies, had not trusted him'. Muriel's experience is likewise partitioned, but in her case between what she can safely examine and what she must stifle. Instinct tells her that the necessity she experiences 'never to examine, brood, or make emotional profit-and-loss accounts about the sex she had with Frederick was healthy. For as soon as she did put weight on that area, start to measure and weigh, all sorts of sensations hitherto foreign to this relationship began to gabble and gobble, insist and demand. Guilt for one.'[18] She advances like a woman balancing a book on her head, fearful of looking down.

Culture Against Man

It is often assumed that disappointment, as experienced by Barnes's and Lessing's characters in their erotic lives, is intrinsic to the sexual act itself. Freud took this view. 'It is easy to show', he once claimed, 'that the value the mind sets on erotic needs instantly sinks as soon as satisfaction becomes readily obtainable. Some obstacle is necessary to swell the tide of the libido to its height.' He also entertained the thought that 'something in the nature of the sexual instinct is unfavourable to the achievement of absolute gratification'.[19] Subsequently, there arose a school of thought which sought to reconcile Freud's views with those of Marx. Among the reconcilers, Marcuse operated at the level of grand theory, while others, like the anthropologist Jules Henry, did so in terms of fieldwork and everyday observation. Both believed that it was society, not biology, which acted to stunt the individual's capacity for pleasure.

In *Eros and Civilization* and *One-Dimensional Man*, Marcuse dwelt explicitly on the repressive effects of the sublimation that society requires of its citizens. He maintained that the desexualisation of the body and the confinement of erotic pleasure to the genitals was a precondition for transforming the body into an instrument of labour. More subtly, however, Marcuse also spoke of 'repressive desublimation', seeing capitalism as a system within which sexual excitement is *managed*.[20] Individuals are thus diverted from those exercises of the imagination in which the erotic suffuses the whole body and mind. They are also neutralised politically; willing, indeed eager, to fulfil their role as consumers.

Capitalism creates a society, Marcuse believed, which 'turns everything it touches into a potential source of progress *and* exploitation'. Banished is the art – from Racine's *Phèdre* to Tolstoy's *Anna Karenina* – in which the expression of the erotic is indirect, but in which the influence of the erotic is 'absolute, uncompromising, unconditional'. Gone is the world in which Balzac could say of the whore Esther that 'hers was the tenderness which blossoms only in infinity'. In its place, Marcuse finds 'O'Neill's alcoholics and Faulkner's savages', the 'stories of Hollywood and New York orgies, and the adventures of suburban housewives'. These are 'wild and obscene', but, for just this reason, 'perfectly harmless'.[21]

In *Culture Against Man*, Jules Henry adopts a more documentary approach, bringing various facets of American culture under review: advertising, education, teenage culture, the treatment of the old, attitudes towards the insane.[22] He rehearses, for example, the advertisers' approach to the problems of ageing skin: '. . . *all new* Angel Skin, used faithfully and frequently every day, will work positive wonders in warding off that hated "old hands" look. *Penetressence* is the reason. *Penetressence* is Pond's own lovely secret . . . an exclusive concentrate of age-defying moisturizers, softeners, and secret essences that go *deep down where ageing begins!*' (The idea of 'penetressence' lingers discomfortingly in the mind, an amalgam of penetration and putrescence.) The 'pecuniary philosophy' implicit in such copy is already at work, Henry notes, within the classroom. In a high school he visits – 'Rome High' – a Mrs Elphin has come to talk to the home economics class of fourteen year olds about wool. On the walls are Helena Rubenstein and Bobbie Brooks advertisements, and a poster on 'Facts About Perspiration'; in a corner, in front of a three-sided mirror, one of the students who, with the assistance of two friends, has been primping herself since the class began. Mrs Elphin moves quickly from the history of sheep farming to the tactics and strategies of shopping: 'Don't buy a dress if you find the same pattern in the yard-goods department', she urges, 'because soon everyone else will have it and they'll be *dirty, untidy, cheap* people, and you'll be so unhappy!'

Henry also describes an evening spent at the local 'Teen Town': a dance hall run by the YMCA. Some two hundred boys and girls are flinging each other around the dance floor; the garments of the girls 'very tight' and the music 'very frenzied, very erotic, almost hypnotic'. Yet, as he describes it, teenage fun is the expression less of pleasure than of anxiety. Since the 1950s and 1960s, of course, adolescent mores have evolved, but the force of Henry's analysis persists; especially his insistence that enterprises like Teen Towns spring up both because they accommodate the anxieties of the young, *and* because they feed the adult economy. Teen Towns, he estimates, were at that time contributing nearly four billion dollars a year to America's gross national product.

Implicit in Henry's analysis there are three elements: (a) a sense of rootlessness or *anomie*; (b) the need to express violent or dissociated impulses; and (c) the commercial exploitation of that need. When in a state of rootlessness, this model assumes, individuals are drawn towards violent or arbitrary action, whether in the realms of sex, sport, drink, drugs, music or gang war, the hallmark of such impulses being their 'split', dissociated quality. In such a state, the individual is ripe for commercial exploitation, willing to pay uncritically for whatever experience currently presents itself as imperative. But in the world of make-believe such transactions establish, each purchase widens the gap between fantasy and everyday reality on which the sense of *anomie* depends. Henry's teenagers are as a consequence mechanistic even in their view of themselves. When they ask 'How do I get a good personality?', they are asking a question strictly analogous to the questions 'How do I grow big breasts? . . . or big biceps?' 'How do I remove the spots on my face? . . . get myself a car?' As Steven Marcus has remarked, 'from organs and objects it is but one step to machines'.[23]

The model implicit in Henry's research is self-fuelling, in other words. Its three elements form a vicious circle:

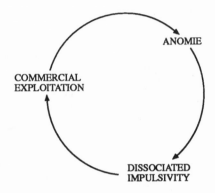

Disappointment

The hidden assumptions governing teenage consumption follow the individual into adult life, and immersion in the fantasy world of brand-names and logos becomes progressively deeper. To an extent that advertisers understand, but their public frequently does not, brands – from washing powders to sports cars – have 'identities'; quasi-personal properties which the copywriter is free to manipulate.[24] These identities influence not only the acquisition of items of hardware, but the creation of a 'lifestyle', citizens becoming consumers of their own desires.

While commercially satisfactory, such a regime carries with it the risk of habitual disappointment: what we find when we have unwrapped our purchases is not what we wish to find. The magic has evaporated. Common sense says that, having been disappointed several times, we will cease to purchase; or at least that we will be increasingly less likely to do so with stars in our eyes. But, as the Princeton economic theorist Albert Hirschman has pointed out, under certain conditions disappointment primes the customer to buy again and again; and it is on this surprising consequence of disappointment that the health of the economy depends.

'The world I am trying to understand', Hirschman says, 'is one in which men think they want one thing and then upon getting it, find out to their dismay that they don't want it nearly as much as they thought or don't want it at all and that something else, of which they were hardly aware, is what they really want.'[25] What interests Hirschman particularly is 'the *power* and *vitality*' of this experience.[26] The customer falls in love with a commodity – whether a silk dress or an auto-focusing camera – buys it, is disappointed and, because disappointed, falls in love again. In part at least, we fall in love again in order to reaffirm to ourselves our capacity to be carried away by extravagant emotion; to seize and be seized.

Hirschman's prime concern is with the movement between private consumption and action in the public interest; and his examples are taken, accordingly, from the market-place and from the life of public institutions. The parallels with the erotic life are obvious, nonetheless. 'What often astonishes me', said the anonymous author of *My Secret Life*, the eloquent Victorian chronicle of sexual obsession, 'is my desire to do again everything sexual and erotic which I have already done.' Commenting, Marcus observes that in 'the virtually endless series of repetitions' that characterise what the author calls his 'rutting fits', we can make out an unending search for 'a gratification that does not exist'.[27]

The parallel between the restless search for the perfect purchase and that for the perfect sexual partner is evidently quite close. There is also a more specific respect in which Hirschman's argument relates to our own. While discussing the frustrations of public life, he introduces as an example the case of the citizen in Vichy France, and in doing so poses a paradox. He makes the disconcerting point that 'the sense of excitement and of participation generated under such conditions contrasts with the boredom and feeling of powerlessness often characteristic of political life in a democracy'.[28] It is only when operating behind the lines, illegally and in mortal danger, he suggests, that you experience yourself as fully alive: both engaged and free. In our later chapters, it will be part of our task to show how this paradox bears on intimate experience too.

Lessing's story and Barnes's lead the reader inexorably to the view that there are no neat solutions; and the tendency of analyses as various as those of Marcuse, Henry and Hirschman is to support this. The path followed by the Smiths and Joneses is without question unsatisfactory. It creates romantic yearnings of the kind which were to haunt Frederick; it can leave guilt in its wake as it did for Althea; and it generates the deceptions and self-deceptions that ensnared Muriel. Loving one another less – Jack's recommendation to Graham Hendrick – is no solution, in that it blunts experience rather than channelling it. What is required are not formulae for outlawing extravagant emotion, but a means of preserving its strength and clarity. Finding a 'home' for extravagant emotion within an enduring relationship becomes possible, we are going to argue, only if the relevant activities are seen as *imaginative* and the relevant judgements are seen as *aesthetic*; if intimacy and art are treated as akin.[29] Before we can make this case, however, a major conceptual obstacle must be cleared away.

CHAPTER SIX

Free for All?

SEVERAL ORTHODOXIES HAVE SWEPT through the human sciences in the last seventy-five years; and while dissimilar in many respects, they have been united in one. Marxism, behaviourism, structuralism: each has failed to make sense of close personal relations. By dwelling so insistently on the aberrant and pathological, even psychoanalysis has failed. Human scientists appear drawn to bodies of belief which prevent the truth about our capacity for intimate pleasure and gratification being told. The possibility must exist that – perversely, puritanically – we are drawn to them for just this reason.

Recently, the human sciences have embraced yet another orthodoxy, but this too conforms to the established pattern, in that it prevents any but the most rudimentary forms of intimate fulfilment from seeming real. While appearing radical, it is a conservative body of ideas which undermines any gratification other than the arbitrary and fleeting. In this chapter, we hope to show where the root of this difficulty lies, and how a better conceptual framework might be constructed.

The New Wisdom

For the last three decades, the dominant voices among the philosophers whose thought bears on the human sciences – in France, Michel Foucault and Jacques Derrida; in America, Richard Rorty – have expressed a view that is insistently relativistic.[1] These authors have contributed to a view of knowledge, sometimes called 'poststructural' or 'postmodern', which is now widely accepted among sociologists, anthropologists and social workers –

the young and forward-looking, especially – and has a solid foot-
ing among psychologists, psychiatrists and psychoanalysts. As it
applies to what we can know of one another, this theory of everyday knowledge has four tenets. That:

Judgements of fact and relevance are always dependent on the
interests and values of those making them;

The effect of such interests and values is to create 'perspectives',
from which the individual's perceptions of reality and illusion
derive;

There are never adequate grounds for concluding that the view
afforded from one perspective is more accurate or truthful than
that afforded by another; and

When apparently objective judgements are unpacked or 'decon-
structed', the interests and values of those making them always
shine through.

Springing initially from scholarly studies of history, literature, and
philosophy itself, this new wisdom quickly revealed distinctive virtues. There is no single point of vantage, for example, from which
to judge what is going on inside a marriage. The wife's view
may differ radically from the husband's; and each of their views
may differ from those of children, lovers, relatives, friends, thera-
pists. A marriage, on this argument, becomes an interlocking
system of perspectives; and the search for a single definitive
account is illusory.[2]

It was quickly apparent too, however, that the new wisdom had
a special bearing on society's beliefs about its marginalised and dis-
advantaged members, and when used in this context its character
changed. What had been relativistic became sharply directional,
the deconstructive method now privileging certain perspectives at
the expense of others: typically those of the left at the expense of
the right, the permissive at the expense of the regulatory. It also
favoured explanations couched in terms of power and of 'sexuality'. These were treated, not as irresistible invitations to further
deconstruction, but as explanatory bedrock. As we shall see in a
moment, this shift was to have troublesome consequences.

Marriage and Modernity

One of the few to examine the implications of the new wisdom for
the modern marriage is Anthony Giddens, a psychoanalytically
alert sociologist. In *The Transformation of Intimacy*, Giddens establishes his own position by contrasting it with Foucault's.[3] Within
Foucault's analysis, he argues, 'the only moving forces are power,
discourse and the body'. What Foucault specifically neglects is 'the
nature of love and, in particular, the rise of the ideals of romantic
love'. Giddens advances his own position by coining two notions:
those of 'plastic sexuality' and of the 'pure relationship'. Sexual
desire becomes 'plastic', he argues, in as much as it is a facet of
experience we are at liberty to explore without regard to its reproductive implications; and intimate relationships become 'pure' if
we are free to enter or abandon them in the light of the personal
benefits we see them as affording. We fall in love with, cohabit
with, or reach carnal accommodations with others. We marry
or do not marry. We have children or do not have children – each
as the driving need or passing whim takes us. The fabric of
conventional responsibilities and constraints built into the institution of marriage drops away, and we pursue whatever goals
we choose.

Such a revolution, Giddens observes, 'is not just, or even
primarily, a gender-neutral advance in sexual permissiveness'. It is
a change, 'deep-lying, and irreversible' which grants sexual auto-
nomy to women and to homosexuals, and one which has
revolutionary implications for the institutions of marriage and the
family. The consequence of sexual emancipation is 'the *radical
democratisation* of the personal'; a transformation embracing not
only love affairs and marriages, but friendships and the relations
between parents and children.[4]

The immediate consequences are troubling, Giddens believes:
'at the moment, an emotional abyss has opened up between
the sexes, and one cannot say with any certainty how far it will
be bridged'.[5]

The Attack on the Binary Frame

Adjacent to Giddens's gloomy analysis of marriage is the tendency among its critics to argue that matrimony is an artifice and a strait-jacket. They urge on one another the freedom to explore and experiment; and, in particular, to escape from the binary categories of 'male' and 'female'. Our natures, these critics typically assume, are inherently bisexual; and it is our androgyny that a patriarchal culture is thought to repress.

A recent variation on this urge to escape the binary is the celebration not so much of the hermaphrodite as the transvestite and transsexual. The impulse to cross-dress is seen as reverberating in a telling manner with all other impulses to dissolve category boundaries: those which separate men from women, homosexual from heterosexual, white from black, rulers from ruled. The distinction between male and female is preserved, but becomes the basis for games of reversal and illusion. The transvestite continually recreates the 'third term', Marjorie Garber believes: not a third sex, but a 'mode of articulation, a way of describing a space of possibility'. Transvestism is 'the disruptive element that intervenes, not just a category crisis of male and female, but the crisis of category itself'.[6]

More radical still is the attempt to discuss the phenomena of sex and gender without reference to the body at all. Judith Butler has spoken of the need for bodily categories to be 'denaturalized' and 'resignified', and allowed to proliferate subversively 'beyond the binary frame'.[7] Bodies, on this argument, cease to be physiological systems, and become sites for games in which the supposedly natural formats of heterosexual intimacy are continuously translated and transformed. Authors like Butler thus offer back to heterosexuals the freedom they believe homosexuals of both sexes have achieved. They are encouraged to explore their own capacities for amorous invention, without regard to the coercive influence of a norm.

From our own point of view, just as Giddens's analysis is too pessimistic, so 'hermaphroditic' and 'transvestite' solutions are misplaced. It is not remotely our intention to pillory or stigmatise those whose appetites place them among one or other of the sexual minorities. Nor do we want to belittle those forms of

invention and creativeness which result from the collapse of boundaries, whether of gender or of genres. Equally, it is no part of our
intention to make heterosexual intimacy seem the gratifying enterprise it undoubtedly can be by stressing the extent to which it
includes elements which are hermaphroditic or transsexual. Our
argument, on the contrary, is that:

> Binary patterns of sex and gender give rise of their own accord to
> configurations of similarity and difference that are exceedingly
> subtle: and

> Heterosexual intimacy is in any case imaginatively galvanising pre-
> cisely because those who are party to it see themselves as both
> necessary to one another and irreducibly dissimilar.

The trick – for lack of a better word – is *to harness the potentially
destructive tensions inherent in the relationship of like-with-unlike, and
hence evolve a context which is imaginatively alive.*

'Sexuality'

An obstacle to such an evolution, we want to argue, is the virtually
universal misuse of a crucially placed abstract noun: 'sexuality'.

In the past, 'sexuality' meant something reasonably specific. The
OED offers three meanings, the first of them to modern ears a
little odd:

> The quality of being sexual or having sex (1800);

> Possession of sexual powers, or capability of sexual feelings (1879);

> Recognition of or preoccupation with what is sexual (1848).

Between them, these establish the idea of human beings as
creatures activated by and alert to sexual desire. In the course of
the last decade or two, however, the use of the term has become
increasingly indiscriminate; and as a result – like 'creativity' – it is
now so over-worked as to have been largely drained of specifiable
sense. Questions of biology, gender identity, object choice and
presentation of self are scrambled together and confused.[8] Half-
hidden in current usage there nonetheless lurks an assumption of

significance. Especially in the kinds of context that the new wisdom creates, 'sexuality' now carries with it the belief that, in sexual matters, we must each be free to express ourselves without evaluation or censure. More particularly, it assumes:

That, as sexual beings, our responsibility is to be true to our own needs and natures; and

That in being true, the law of the land aside, we are finally accountable only to ourselves.

The question of tolerance – of live-and-let-live – aside, there are two issues here, neither simple. The first is that of *hedonism*, the impression of sex as a species of natural abundance, a pleasurable cornucopia of the senses; the second, of *solipsism*, the thought that the cornucopia brims over without regard to intimacy or relationship. Both are implicit in Giddens's notion of 'plastic sexuality', and both pose difficulties, the second no less than the first.

Although reformers like Kinsey and his successors have for decades been offering the public vistas of sexual variety and sexual plenty, there is, to the best of our knowledge, no research which shows that sex is more gratifying if (a) conducted often rather than more occasionally, (b) using a wide rather than a restricted range of practices, (c) promiscuously, instead of within an exclusive relationship of mutual trust, or (d) unconstrainedly, without reference to personal, moral or aesthetic values.

Our guess is that, when eventually collected, the evidence will prove complex, and will require us to distinguish between just those facets of erotic experience that the modern usage of 'sexuality' blurs: the sensory experience of sex itself; the thoughts and fantasies immediately associated with that experience; the statistics of rates, partners and practices; and the broader context of attitudes and beliefs within which each sexual act is set. A homosexual man who has forty sexual encounters in a bathhouse in the course of a weekend is sometimes assumed to reach dizzying heights of erotic gratification. Yet the sexual pleasure he actually experiences may only be moderate. What the bathhouse celebrant achieves may not be a very large number of orgasms, nor even a few orgasms of remarkable force or eloquence, but sexual contact which is anonymous, and transporting for that reason. It is also widely assumed that, questions of genital hygiene aside, such an enterprise is liberated and liberating, but it may be so only in the sense that it provides the individual in question with a brief respite from an obsession.

As currently used, the notion of 'sexuality' restricts and distorts the discussion of such events, and does this all the more persuasively because presenting itself as a life-enhancing subversion. As a conceptual entity, it is positively virus-like in its resilience. If you question either its hedonism or its solipsism, you are assumed to be attacking the principle of live-and-let-live. If you question the principle of live-and-let-live on the grounds that some sexual practices are harmful or disgusting, you are assumed to be hostile to pleasure. If you criticise it as part of an attack on pleasure, as we are doing, you are assumed to be eccentric or quirky.

The Solipsists

Easily overlooked in the haste to strike a non-judgemental attitude is the reality of each sexual transaction. There are those, for example, within which one person acts with abandon while the other shrivels internally; both denying to themselves and to one another that this is what is happening. Such binds are captured with greater clarity in fiction than in factual research, Truman Capote's quasi-biographical *Answered Prayers* detailing just such a relationship.

Capote seems first to have entertained *Answered Prayers* in 1966; the year in which, to huge acclaim, he published *In Cold Blood*, his factional account of a psychopathic killing. He planned that it would describe the private lives of the very rich; and he envisaged it as the contemporary equivalent of Proust's *Remembrance of Things Past*. Like *In Cold Blood*, and like Normal Mailer's *The Executioner's Song*, it was to be a species of novel which – in Mailer's phrase – was 'ready to play by the rules of biography'. Capote was free to write *Answered Prayers* out of sequence, he was later to claim, a chapter here a chapter there, because 'the plot – or rather plots – was true, and all the characters were real: it wasn't difficult to keep it all in mind, for I hadn't invented anything'.[9] But it *was* difficult. Three chapters were published in *Esquire* and caused a furore; but, thereafter, while he often spoke of the book as to all

intents finished, nothing more was seen. Witty, compulsively read-
able, and often flamboyantly obscene, these three chapters seem
tacked together in the spirit of a gossip column, scandalous revela-
tions treading on one another's heels in their haste to be heard.

Even so, there is no doubting Capote's capacity to cast human
frailty in a clear light. In the first of his chapters, 'Unspoiled Mon-
sters', he introduces the reader to the literary world seen, as it
were, from below. Through the narrator P. B. Jones, the author's
bisexual doppelgänger, we meet the literary editor Turner Boatwright of the 'chilly crotch-watching eyes'; the 'kind of queer who
has Freon refrigerating his bloodstream', and whose office rocking
chair 'contained a little pillow with an embroidered inscription:
MOTHER'.[10] We also overhear extraordinary exchanges like that
between Greta Garbo and Cecil Beaton, who has taken Jones's
photograph for Boatwright's magazine. 'Beaton: "The most distressing fact of growing older is that I find my private parts are
shrinking." Garbo, after a mournful pause: "Ah, if only I could say
the same."'[11]

We then encounter Alice Lee Langman, the doyenne of
American letters; 'the queen of the writer-in-residence swindle, the
prizes racket, the high-honorarium con, the grants-in-aid-to-strug-
gling artists shit'. She falls in love with Jones. What he wants from
her in return is 'her agent, her publisher, her name attached to a
Holy Roller critique of my work in one of those moldy but academically influential quarterlies'; objectives which were 'in time,
achieved and dazzlingly added to'. Miss Langman ensures that
Jones receives a Guggenheim Fellowship, a grant from the
National Institute of Arts and Letters, and a publisher's advance
for a collection of short stories; ones that she has prepared and
groomed, and then reviewed, once in *Partisan Review* and again in
the *New York Times Book Review*. The title – '*Answered Prayers*' –
was her choice too; a quotation from St Teresa of Avila who
observed that 'More tears are shed over answered prayers than
unanswered ones.' It captures the theme which she sees moving
through Jones's work, as Capote sees it moving through his own:
that of 'people achieving a desperate aim only to have it rebound
upon them – accentuating, and accelerating, their desperation'.[12]

'When I met Miss Langman, and I never called her anything
else, she was far into her late fifties, yet she looked eerily unaltered
from her long-ago Genthe portrait. The author of *Wild Asparagus*

and *Five Black Guitars* had eyes the color of Anatolian waters, and
her hair, a sleek silvery blue, was brushed straight back, fitting her
erect head like an airy cap. Her nose was reminiscent of Pavlova's:
prominent, slightly irregular. She was pale, with a healthy pallor,
an apple-whiteness, and when she spoke she was difficult to understand, for her voice ... was muted, as cello-contralto as a
mourning dove's.'[13]

Jones describes himself as 'one of those persons who, when
sexually immersed, require serious silence, the hush of impeccable
concentration'. 'I am rarely with the person I am with, so to say;
and I'm sure that many of us, even most of us, share this condition
of dependence upon an inner scenery, imagined and remembered
erotic fragments, shadows irrelevant to the body above or beneath
us – those images our minds accept inside sexual seizure but
exclude once the beast has been routed, for, regardless of how
tolerant we are, these cameos are intolerable to the mean-spirited
watchmen within us.' If he is 'to reach an edge and fall over', he
says, 'all the mechanics must be assisted by the deepest fantasizing,
an intoxicating mental cinema that does not welcome lovemaking
chatter'. Miss Langman, in contrast, was 'indeed a talker: a
relentless bedroom back-seat driver' ... '"That's better better and
better Billy let me have billy now that's uh uh uh it that's *it* only
slower slower and slower now hard hard hit it hard ay ay *los cojones*
let me hear them ring now slower slower dradraaaaagdrag it out
now hit hard hard ay ay daddy Jesus have mercy Jesus Jesus god-
damdaddyamighty come with me Billy come, come."' 'How can
I', Jones reasonably asks, 'when the lady won't let me concentrate
on areas more provocative than her roaring roiling undisciplined
persona? "Let's hear it, let's hear them ring": thus the grande
mademoiselle of the cultural press as she bucked her way through
a sixty-second sequence of multiple triumphs.' Jones then goes off
to the bathroom, and, stretched out in the cold dry bathtub,
thinks the thoughts necessary to him, just as Miss Langman, 'in
the private quietude beneath her public turbulence, had been
absorbed in hers'.[14]

On his return, Miss Langman thanks him. 'I had thought I was
accepting a pupil', she says, 'but it would seem he has nothing to
learn.' This last sentence the narrator describes as 'stylistically
characteristic – direct, felt, yet a bit *enunciated*, literary'.[15] Yet 'she
was in love with me, she said so, and I believed her; one night,

when her voice waved and dipped from too much red and yellow wine, she asked – oh in such a whimper-simper stupid-touching way you wanted to knock out her teeth but maybe kiss her, too – whether I loved her; as I'm naught if not a liar, I told her sure'.[16]

In the end, Jones leaves Miss Langman in the lurch; and carries with him the memory of 'her sitting there in her perfect-taste parlor, with gin and tears reddening her beautiful eyes, nodding, nodding, nodding, absorbing every word of my mean gin-inspired assaults ... biting her lips, suppressing any hint of retaliation, accepting it because she was as strong in the sureness of her gifts as I was feeble and paranoid in the uncertainty of mine, and because she knew one swift true sentence from her would be lethal'. She would lose him; and, with him, her last fling at love.[17] (But to lose Jones and her last fling at love, was by no means to give up sex. Miss Langman would remain 'an enthusiast', Jones observes, 'until a stroke killed her'.)

While it may be tempting to dismiss Capote's depiction of Miss Langman as the product of misogyny, to see it solely in these terms is to miss its bearing both on the nature of close relationships and on currently popular assumptions about them. For here we see the segregation of sexual experience into facets, each of which can in practice operate independently (love, desire, talk about desire in general, talk about desire as part of the sexual act, the 'intoxicating mental cinema'); and the fact that someone who, beyond question, has 'discovered her own sexuality', is blind to her lover's needs and frailties – and, it might be argued, is blind because that discovery has been made.

Miss Langman brings to mind Jacques Lacan's dictum that 'there is no such thing as a sexual relationship.'[18] More specifically, her attitude is *non-reciprocal*. She loves P. B. Jones and assumes that she knows what he does and thinks, but does not. Nor would it cross her mind to find out. The men – and, it is intimated, women – who share her bed are of sexual significance to her only in as much as they meet her private needs as she roars and roils her way to another 'multiple triumph'. There is no hint that, in her excitement, one mind opens to another; still less that there might be moments when the other's gratification holds more meaning for her than her own. The solipsistic tendency inherent in her cast of mind is one that a deconstructive philosophy tends to concentrate and intensify; and it does so by undermining just those paths that Miss Langman might reasonably be expected to follow, were she to seek a clearer understanding of what P. B. Jones was actually thinking and doing, either when in bed with her, or in her bathtub afterwards. Any such search is futile, it insists. The notion of access to what P. B. Jones was actually thinking and doing is illusory. We might accurately record his actions with a hidden video camera, but we would have no knowledge of what these meant. We are precluded from such knowledge because, like Jones himself, we have no access to his unconscious mental processes – and even if we did, we would discover them to be ambiguous. Rather than being a receptacle for true meanings, the unconscious is, to use Malcolm Bowie's phrase, an 'extraordinary agent of dispersal and surprise'.[19]

In place of knowledge, the new wisdom offers a vision: that of a kaleidoscopic multiplicity of erotic perspectives – within each life and within each sexual act. The elements of this multiplicity are fuelled by desire (or 'sexuality'); and its paradigmatic expression is to be found in the chance encounter – either with a stranger, or with a hitherto undisclosed facet of a personality previously assumed to be familiar. Lust blazes for a moment, transfixes us, and is then extinguished; the other remaining someone who is in all essentials unknown and unknowable. While it is the crassest of errors to discuss philosophical doctrines exclusively in terms of the private needs of those who invent them, it is presumably no accident that Foucault, one of the begetters of the new wisdom, should have engaged in homosexual sado-masochism and bathhouse encounters.[20]

At extremes, these theoreticians deny that there is any such thing as a person, or a brain – and, if they are consistent, any such thing as a culture or a text. What they offer in the place of the *bêtes humaines* of sociobiology are sites of consciousness, evanescently structured in the light of perspectives and their attendant assumptions; and in place of intimacy, the concordances (or illusions of concordance) that such perspectives and assumptions from time to time allow.

Private Conversations

On the other hand, as Rorty himself insists, philosophers are not legislators, still less representatives of a thought-police. Erotic intimacies that endure and engross are facts of life. As Robert Stoller remarks and the survey evidence tends to confirm, there are couples for whom familiarity produces not less pleasure but greater pleasure.[21] If it is to accommodate such realities, a philosophical formulation must incorporate two thoroughly un-postmodern properties. It must allow:

For distinctions between what *appears to be* and what *is*.

It must accommodate clear and sustainable distinctions between what Miss Langman chose to believe P. B. Jones was thinking and doing, and what he was actually thinking and doing. And, it must allow:

The insights afforded by two vantage points to *converge*.

It must admit that P. B. Jones and Miss Langman could in principle have reached a more accurate and more imaginatively fertile understanding of one another than in fact they did.

If we are to make sense of the phenomena of erotic intimacy, we must countenance forms of knowledge-generation that, like conversations, can:

Get somewhere worth getting; yet

Remain in principle inconclusive.

In turn, this approach revitalises preoccupations that the new wisdom has encouraged a generation of psychologists to neglect:

The question of *subjective value* – of what each party to a close relationship perceives as precious;

The phenomena of *empathy* and the extent, more generally, to which one person can share another's thought and feeling; and

The distinction within a close relationship between what is acknowledged and unacknowledged, between *legal traffic and contraband*.[22]

Also congruent with this view is the parallel between the world of close relations and that of art.[23] It is this parallel that shapes what we have to say in the rest of the book. In the next chapter, we will show how turbulent emotion, and especially turbulent emotion concerning those we desire, is translated into art. The life and work are seen as the twin elements of a system which exists, typically, in a state of precarious equilibrium.

Chapter 8 then deals more schematically with the nature of this parallel between intimacy and art, emphasising those facets of human need and intelligence that a psychology of the aesthetic response must accommodate. A simple diagrammatic model is proposed, applicable to works of art and intimacy alike, in which the properties of control and uncertainty are combined. In our last chapter, in contrast, we offer a conjecture: a psychological view of the origin of moral values, and of the role these values play in erotic experience.

CHAPTER SEVEN

Life and Art

MARGUERITE DURAS'S *THE LOVER* is a short novel, apparently autobiographical.[1] Its setting is Indo-China between the world wars; and it describes the sexual relationship of a French adolescent girl with a somewhat older man. The heroine's mother is an eccentric school teacher; her father, off-stage throughout, is dying or already dead. She has two brothers: the older, a scrounger and brute; the younger more fragile, and later to die of bronchial pneumonia during the Japanese occupation. The girl's lover is Chinese; in prospect at least formidably rich, but for reasons of race and personality despised. It may be that Duras's vision of her own sex is excessively severe or idiosyncratic. Her narrative indicates, nevertheless, that the obstacles to heterosexual intimacy lie as much in the perversities and contradictions of the female psyche as in those of the male.[2]

The girl and her lover first meet en route for Saigon, as the girl is going back to boarding school. 'I often think', the girl recalls, 'of the image only I can see now, and of which I've never spoken. It's always there, in the same silence, amazing. It's the only image of myself I like, the only one in which I recognise myself, in which I delight' . . . 'So, I'm fifteen and a half. It's on a ferry crossing the Mekong river. The image lasts all the way across.'[3]

It is a scene set in terms of appearances, the girl's face and apparel: 'At the age of fifteen I had the face of pleasure, and yet I had no knowledge of pleasure. There was no mistaking that face. Even my mother must have seen it. My brothers did. That was how everything started for me – with that flagrant, exhausted face, those rings round the eyes, in advance of time and experience' . . . 'I'm wearing a dress of real silk, but it's threadbare, almost transparent. It used to belong to my mother. One day she decided the colour was too bright for her and she gave it to me. It's a sleeveless dress with a very low neck. It's the sepia colour real silk takes

on with wear. It's a dress I remember. I think it suits me. I'm
wearing a leather belt with it, perhaps a belt belonging to one of
my brothers' . . . 'This particular day I must be wearing the
famous pair of gold lamé high heels' . . . 'Bargains, final reductions
bought for me by my mother' . . . 'It's not the shoes, though, that
make the girl look so strangely, so weirdly dressed. No, it's the
fact that she's wearing a man's flat-brimmed hat, a brownish pink
fedora with a broad black ribbon. The crucial ambiguity of the
image lies in the hat' . . . 'No woman, no girl wore a man's fedora
in that colony then. No native woman either' . . . 'Suddenly I see
myself as another, as another would be seen, outside myself, available to all, available to all eyes, in circulation for cities, journeys,
desire. Having got it, this hat that all by itself makes me whole, I
wear it all the time. With the shoes it must have been much the
same, but after the hat. They contradict the hat, as the hat contradicts the puny body, so they're right for me.'[4]

'On the ferry, look, I've still got my hair. Fifteen and a half. I'm
using make-up already. I use Crème Tokalon, and try to camou-
flage the freckles on my cheeks, under the eyes. On top of the
Crème Tokalon I put natural-colour powder – Houbignant. The
powder's my mother's, she wears it to go to government recep-
tions. That day I've got lipstick on too, dark red, cherry, as the
fashion was then' . . . 'On the ferry, beside the bus, there's a big
black limousine with a chauffeur in white cotton livery' . . . 'Inside
the limousine there's a very elegant man looking at me. He's not a
white man. He's wearing European clothes – the light tussore suit
of the Saigon bankers. He's looking at me. I'm used to people
looking at me.'[5]

Not only do these clothes come from her mother, the girl wears
them with her mother in mind. 'My mother, my love, her incredible ungainliness, with her cotton stockings darned by Dô, in the
tropics she still thinks you have to wear stockings to be a lady, a
headmistress, her dreadful shapeless dresses, mended by Dô, she's
still straight out of her Picardy farm full of female cousins, thinks
you ought to wear everything till it's worn out, that you have to
be deserving, her shoes, her shoes are down-at-heel, she walks
awkwardly, painfully, her hair's drawn back tight into a bun like a
Chinese woman's, we're ashamed of her, I'm ashamed of her in the
street outside the school, when she drives up to the school in her
old Citroen B12 everyone looks, but she, she doesn't notice anything, ever, she ought to be locked up, beaten, killed. She looks at

me and says: Perhaps you'll escape. Day and night this obsession. It's not that you have to achieve anything, it's that you have to get away from where you are. When my mother emerges, comes out of her despair, she sees the man's hat and the gold lamé shoes. She asks what's it all about. I say nothing. She looks at me, is pleased, smiles' ... 'She must think it's a good sign, this show of imagination, the way the girl's thought of dressing like this. She not only accepts this buffoonery, this unseemliness, she, sober as a widow, dressed in dark colours like an unfrocked nun, she not only accepts it, she likes it.'[6]

The impact of her ensemble, the narrator stresses, is instantaneous; for the perceived no less than the perceiver. 'You didn't have to attract desire. Either it was in the woman who aroused it or it didn't exist. Either it was there at first glance or else it had never been. It was instant knowledge of sexual relationship or it was nothing. That too I knew before I experienced it.'[7] She also knows, more or less from the first moment, that the Chinese man is at her mercy, and that others will be too, should the occasion arise. The time has come, she recognises, 'when she can no longer escape certain duties towards herself. And that her mother will know nothing of this, nor her brothers. She knows this now too. As soon as she got into the black car she knew: she's excluded from the family for the first time and for ever' ... 'Now the child will have to reckon only with this man, the first, the one who introduced himself on the ferry.'[8]

There ensues a love affair of daily assignations in a flat rented for the purpose. He loves her; she does not love him. Indeed, she tells him she doesn't want him to talk; she wants him to do to her what he usually does with the women he brings to the flat. 'She begs him to do that.' Eventually, the girl introduces her impoverished mother and brothers to the man, who takes them out to eat luxuriously. The brothers gorge themselves, but neither they nor their mother address a word to their host. The family is unified in its contempt. Eighteen months later, the mother takes the daughter with her back to France; and, by then, the affair has lost its momentum. The man is there to bid her a silent goodbye, hidden in his limousine, parked at a safe distance from the European well-wishers on the quay.

When the girl leaves her lover, it is apparently without regret. Through him and her sexual connection with him, she has begun to negotiate her separation from her depressed and disorderly mother, her loathsome elder brother, her frail younger brother. In as much as she would subsequently recover more tender feelings towards him, she would do so inadvertently, in the interstices of a life that has quite different purposes. He, on the other hand, remains in her thrall. Many years later, he makes contact with her, and tells her that he loves her and always will.

La Douleur

The Lover is a salutary tale, in that it punctures popular misconceptions about the inherent nature of women's capacity for warmth, closeness and compassion. More important, it strips sex not only of intimacy but of physical passion, portraying the young woman's erotic preoccupations as self-regarding, narcissistic. She enters the sexual arena in order to establish herself as separate; and does this by means of a sustained campaign of passivity and rejection towards a man who is in her power.

The Lover was to have a sequel of sorts; one which deals with Duras's narrator as a young married woman. In *La Douleur*, Duras gives a harrowing account of the months in which women like herself waited for their men to return to Paris from the Nazi concentration camps.[9] Her life is organised around 'Robert L.'s' chances of surviving, her thoughts of death, his eventual return, and the appalling physical condition he proves to be in, close to death and barely escaping it. There are dreadful accounts of his excrement: green, slimy, bubbling. Only as the narrative unfolds do we gather that Robert is in fact her husband. Towards the end, as he regains strength, she records that she tells him two painful truths. That his younger sister did not survive. And then, more or less in the same breath, that they must divorce because she must marry 'D.' and have his child.

The narrator says that she will always weep at the mention of Robert's name, and will do so even if he is sitting beside her, smiling back at her as he catches her eye. 'It was then, by his deathbed', she says, 'that I knew him, Robert L., best, that I understood forever what made him himself, himself alone and nothing and no one else in the world'.[10] With every hour of every day, she thinks – and will go on thinking – 'He didn't die in the concentration camp.' Yet the relation of this discovery to her rejection of Robert is offered enigmatically. She is neither guilty nor reparative. She has undergone violent and apparently inconsistent needs, and she records them baldly. The implication is that she could make contact with her husband, and do so in the context of heartfelt love and care, only because their marriage was void. Its threads had been dropped, and a fresh start was to be made elsewhere. Recognition of the 'other's otherness' is possible, Duras implies, only in the absence of intimacy; conversely, intimacy is sustainable only as long as real contact is not made.

Marguerite Duras's method is as simple as it is unsettling. She confronts the reader with the experience of the narrator confronting herself. Where an author like Norman Mailer leaves the reader asking 'But what did Gary Gilmore *really* think, *really* feel?', Duras faces us with the thought that there is nothing more to find out.[11] Beyond the violence of its circumstances, what is shocking about *La Douleur* is not the author's failure to make sense of its narrator on our behalf; but her failure even to try. She writes without obligation to regulate and domesticate the seemingly arbitrary discontinuities which close relationships contain, or to place these within a framework that her readers will find intelligible. Intimate experience *is* arbitrary, she seems to be saying, and the conventions of narrative and characterisation are extraneous to it. They are devices we use to protect ourselves from the embarrassment our arbitrarinesses would otherwise cause.

The developmental sequence implicit in *The Lover* and *La Douleur* is the reverse, then, of the one on which commonsense and popular psychology rely. First, there is the magnetic power to attract, and the narcissistic fascination associated with that power. Next, there are hostile sentiments (in her heroine's case, passivity and rejection); qualities expressed in the heart of the sexual act, and driven steadily into the consciousness of the enamoured male. Only much later does the young woman begin to separate herself from her mother, and become capable of sustaining an intimacy in her own right. Even then, as *La Douleur* shows, her performance is deeply equivocal. When that young woman looks inwards, she finds nothing: 'The story of my life doesn't exist. Does not exist. There's never any centre to it. No path, no line. There are great spaces where you pretend there used to be someone, but it's not true, there was no one.'[12]

The question of whether, at any point, the young woman experiences sexual pleasure is, from Duras's point of view, an irrelevance. It is poignant memories that constitute the nodes of substance in this uncentred enterprise: the memory of waiting for Robert L., the recollection of herself on the Mekong ferry in fedora hat and golden lamé shoes.

Writing it Down

From the outset, the fictional narrator of *The Lover* was intent on being a *writer*: 'Fifteen and a half. The body's thin, undersized almost, childish breasts still, red and pale pink make-up. And then the clothes, the clothes that might make people laugh, but don't. I can see it's all there. All there, but nothing yet done. I can see it in the eyes, all there already in the eyes. I want to write. I've already told my mother: That's what I want to do – write. No answer the first time. Then she asks: Write what? I say: Books, novels. She says grimly: When you've got your maths degree you can write if you like, it won't be anything to do with me then. She's against it, it's not worthy, it's not real work, it's nonsense. Later she said: A childish idea.'[13]

Like her heroine, Duras wrote about her own experience. Where, as fiction, *The Lover* has a complex relationship to Duras's life, *La Douleur* is immediately autobiographical. She wrote it cathartically, as if carrying out a therapeutic exercise recommended by her psychoanalyst. 'I found this diary', she says in introduction, 'in a couple of exercise books in the blue cupboards at Neauphle-le-Château. I have no recollection of having written it. I know I did, I know it was I who wrote it. I recognise my own hand-writing and the details of the story. I can see the place, the Gare d'Orsay, and the various comings and goings. But I can't see myself writing the diary. When would I have done so, in what year, at what times of day, in what house? I can't remember. One thing is certain: it is inconceivable to me that I could have written it while I was actually awaiting Robert L.'s return. How could I have written this thing I still can't put a name to, and that appalls me when I reread it? And how could I have left it lying for years in a house in the country that's regularly flooded in winter? The first time I thought about it was when the magazine *Sorcières* asked me for a text I'd written when I was young. *La Douleur* is one of the most important things in my life. It can't really be called "writing". I found myself looking at pages regularly filled with small, calm, extraordinarily even handwriting. I found myself confronted with a tremendous chaos of thought and feeling that I couldn't bring myself to tamper with, and beside which literature was something of which I felt ashamed.'[14]

The distinction between truth and invention is clear to her mind, as her comment on another of her stories in the same collection shows: 'This one is invented. Literature' . . . 'I have rewritten it. Now I can't remember what it's about. But it's a text that takes off on its own. It might work well in the movies.'[15] It has its own momentum, she plainly feels, and it might do well as her filmscript for *Hiroshima Mon Amour* had done. In contrast, *La Douleur* tells the truth; and, beside it, even the small element of invention in a work like *The Lover* becomes a source of unease.

Published in 1984, *The Lover* proved hugely popular and won the Prix Goncourt. It presumably did so because it allows just enough slippage between the literal and the invented to provide room for the empathising reader. *La Douleur* is briefer, harsher, and casts something of a chill. It stands so close to life that – like black-and-white photographs of the concentration camps – it seems not so much a recreation of suffering as suffering itself. From the writer's point of view, however, there is a distinction to be drawn. Her recollections of waiting for her husband's return are one thing; reading her own diary is another. The first is over-laid by other memories, and is muted by the effects of emotional fatigue and denial; yet at the same time its influence seeps into other areas of her experience and discolours them. Her diary, in contrast, carries her back to the heart of that experience, and at the same time – by being written down – contains it.[16]

The translation of unruly experience into black words on a white page serves, simultaneously, both to distill turbulent emotion and to distance it. What is true of writers is true of painters, and also in their own ways of photographers and actors. The nature of the psychological manoeuvres implicit in the translation of life into art will differ in detail from medium to medium and genre to genre – from the novel to poetry, and from painting to photography, even from black-and-white photography to colour. But if our theorising is correct, the translation will act in each case both to clarify and to regulate; and will tend to take 'female' and 'male' forms. There is always the risk, too, that in the end translation will devour the translator. Writers can find that they experience emotion vividly only when turning it into words; photographers and painters that they can see clearly only what they transform into a two-dimensional image. Between bouts of work, they are creatures in abeyance, waiting for the juices to stir.

Naked Women in Locked Rooms

Walter (later Richard) Sickert is a painter whose reputation has recently undergone radical revision. Once the focus of scandal, he had come to be seen as a stalwart of the English School, who painted street scenes of Dieppe, recorded the life of the music halls, and left behind him a large body of felicitous line drawings and etchings. His attitudes and sensibilities were assumed to be those of a late Victorian or Edwardian; and he was known to have been something of a card. Only lately has it been rediscovered that, throughout his career, he possessed a distinctive capacity to disturb.

Sickert was born in Munich in 1860; his father a Danish painter and illustrator, his mother the illegitimate daughter of an English astronomer and an Irish dancer. The family came to England when young Walter was eight. Academically able, he considered a career in the British Museum Library, but turned this down on grounds of expense and, instead, fell back on his gifts as an actor, working on the stage for two years under the pseudonym 'Mr Nemo'. At the age of nineteen, he met Whistler, whom he very much admired; and on holiday in France with his family, Oscar Wilde.[17]

By now painting occasionally, he started a year's course at the Slade; but soon left to become Whistler's pupil and assistant. In 1883, while still in his early twenties, he travelled to Paris on Whistler's behalf, with letters of introduction to both Degas and Manet. Manet was too ill to see him, but Degas showed him his studio; and Sickert formed a friendship with the older man which endured.

In 1886, Sickert had his first one-man exhibition, still as a pupil of Whistler; but by 1888 was exhibiting in his own right. At the New English Art Club show of that year, one of his two submissions, *Gatti's Hungerford Palace of Varieties: Second Turn of Miss Katie Lawrence*, shared pride of place with Wilson Steer's *Summer Evening*, and created a furore. The controversy it provoked was more heated, in fact, than any surrounding an English painting of the late nineteenth century. Gatti's was known as a haunt of prostitutes; and Sickert's depiction of Katie, famous for serio-comic songs like 'Daisy Bell', was felt to be grotesque. One critic saw it as 'the lowest degradation of which the art of painting is capable'; another as embodying 'the aggressive squalor which pervades to a greater or lesser extent the whole of modern existence'.[18]

Subsequently, Sickert produced many images of music halls; and most have the same capacity to unsettle. What Sickert did, and what his critics found offensive, was to treat his subject-matter in a way which emphasised not its vitality but its seediness. Under his brush, scenes are drained of their excitement, and turned into awkward marks and gestures. Most eloquent of all in this respect is the texture of the paint itself. Sickert's canvases were smeared and crusted with paint that brings inescapably to mind the thought of *grime*: the waste that gathers on the surfaces of slum buildings, sometimes warmly faecal, but more often cold, inert. This effect persisted even when, in the 1920s, his palate lightened. His colours became bright, sometimes acrid, but the seediness lingered.

When Sickert was still in his twenties, Degas had showed him his pastels of nude women which were in two respects revolutionary. Rather than being posed as set pieces for the spectator's inspection, the women in question are spied on, as through a key-hole. They are also depicted not as foci of erotic fascination or disgust, but as living entities which, in their own right, deserved translation into the language of art. It was not until he was in his forties that Sickert himself began to paint nudes; but when he did, the vision which had earlier preoccupied Degas took a new turn. For while Degas's women have about them an air of nobility, what Sickert depicts is low life with its last pretence of glamour removed: prostitutes in dreary rooms, sometimes with clients, sometimes alone.

'But now let us strip Tilly Pullen of her lendings', Sickert wrote at the time, 'and tell her to put her own things on again. Let her leave the studio and climb the first dirty little staircase in the first shabby little house. Tilly Pullen becomes interesting at once. She is in surroundings that mean something. She becomes stuff for a picture. Follow her into the kitchen, or, better still – for the artist has the divine privilege of omnipresence – into her bedroom; and Tilly Pullen is become the stuff of which the Parthenon was made, of Dürer, or any Rembrandt. She is become a Degas or Renoir, and stuff for the draughtsman.' 'Perhaps the chief source of pleasure in the aspect of a nude', he also wrote, 'is that it is in the nature of a gleam – a gleam of light and warmth and life'.[19]

Sickert's method was to hire a bedroom, and shut himself up inside it with his model. (As well as painting her, the assumption is that he also had sexual intercourse with her. What in fact happened between Sickert and his models, however, remains mysterious, the evidence about his private life being – like Degas's – thin.) At one level, Sickert's nudes epitomise the prostitute's relation to her clients – and, more generally perhaps, Sickert's view of the relation of one sex to the other: 'lassitude, boredom, a dusty truce, a few words'.[20] A painting like *La Hollandaise* is also shocking in its brutality, though; and it was to exert a formative influence on British painters of the next generation: Francis Bacon, Frank Auerbach, David Bomberg. Many of these nudes of Sickert's were seen as pornographic, and were sent abroad to be sold. They have nothing to do with amorous titillation.[21]

Like many Britons, Sickert was deeply taken with Jack the Ripper's crimes; a case closely tied in the popular imagination to thoughts of corruption in high places. The Duke of Clarence, Edward VII's son and the heir apparent, was thought to be implicated; and so too was Sir William Gull, Queen Victoria's ageing physician-in-ordinary. Recently, a number of authors have sought to implicate Sickert himself; even to unmask him as the Ripper. Those with expert knowledge of Sickert's biography – Wendy Baron, for example, and Richard Shone – dismiss such claims out of hand. There is no solid evidence, they point out, which links Sickert either to the murders of the five prostitutes or to Clarence. Such linkage as there is derives from a Mr Joseph

Gorman, who took the name 'Sickert'; claimed to be Sickert's illegitimate son; and put it about that Sickert had revealed detailed knowledge to him of the Ripper crimes.

On the grounds of chronology alone, the notion of Sickert-as-the-Ripper is, it seems, highly implausible. But such scholarly objections do little to stem the tide of speculation; and one has only to stand in the presence of Sickert's collected works to see why. They bring together the idea of squalor with that of dissimulation; and do so with particular force in the context of the naked female body. The impact of these works is all the more impressive because so obviously the product of a highly refined visual intelligence.

In the Camden Town murder, a decade later, the prostitute Emily Dimmock was found naked in bed in her lodgings with her throat cut. Robert Wood, a commercial artist, stood trial for the crime but, defended by Marshall Hall, was acquitted. Sickert's attitude towards the murder seems to have compounded ghoulish curiosity with an oddly dissociated sense of the comic; and he used it to identify and characterise a series of nudes he was doing at the time. In these, a naked woman lies on a bed with a fully clothed man sitting beside her; and the canvases are given jocose titles like *Summer Afternoon or What shall we do for the Rent?* At no point do these images depict violence, except by the most indirect means. But an air of brutality is present, and it is achieved by the conjunction of Sickert's subject-matter – clothed men and naked women – with certain alarming distortions of the body, and with a paint surface calculated to deny the eye even the most rudimentary sensory satisfaction. Like *Gatti's*, the Camden Town murder sequence shocked a number of the artist's colleagues; and one, Fred Brown, professor of painting at the Slade, found it so sordid that he felt compelled to break off their friendship.

There is no doubt that Sickert was odd. Intermittently, he would shave his head and face completely; curious in itself, this change altered his appearance categorically, the bohemian artist disappearing to be replaced by a figure urbanely elegant, even Prussian – an impresario, say, or a diplomat. He married three times; on the second occasion, scarcely knowing who his wife was. In his mid-sixties, following a serious illness, he changed not only his style of painting but also his name, abandoning 'Walter' and adopting his second name 'Richard'. In old age, he bellowed imprecations, and stamped around in what the novelist Denton Welch took to be sewer boots. He became 'the legendary Sickert "of the uproarious music-halls, the wit, the party man, the actor"; the Sickert of outrageous *canards* and impossible clothes, who loved London for its "Evil racy little faces (and) the whiff of leather and stout from the swing-doors of pubs"; the man for whom taxis and telegrams seem to have been invented'. He was 'the Richard Sickert PRBA, ARA, who hung a print of Landseer's *Monarch of the Glen* in his studio "*pour emmerder*" Roger Fry'; yet who both laughed uproariously and wept at Fry's funeral.[22]

One of the more curious features of Sickert's eccentricity concerned lavatories. Throughout his career as a critic, he spoke in favour of earthy vigour and earthy values: 'The plastic arts are gross arts', he wrote in 1910, 'dealing joyously with gross material facts. They call, in their servants, for a robust stomach and a great power of endurance, and while they will flourish in the scullery, or on the dunghill, they fade at a breath from the drawing-room.'[23] As a young man, he is said to have been obsessive about personal cleanliness; but in later life, this changed. After his illness and his marriage to his third wife, the painter Thérèse Lessore, he instructed the builders to remove the conventional lavatory bowls from their newly acquired house in Islington, and to replace them with French floor pans – in order, he said, to see his visitors' faces as they emerged and when necessary to rush to the aid of distressed lady guests.[24] Lavatories featured, too, in Denton Welch's recollection of Sickert. He and a friend had gone to visit Lessore and Sickert at their house in St Peter's near Margate. They found that the entrance to the house was made through what had previously been a downstairs lavatory: 'I remember with vividness the slight shock I received on being confronted with a glistening white "WC" as soon as the door was opened. Mrs. Sickert stood beside it, welcoming us charmingly, with great quietness.'[25]

It was in shocks of this kind that Sickert had all his life specialised. He administered them in his paintings of Katie Lawrence at Gatti's, and of the Camden Town murder, and was administering them still in his old age, both in his paintings and in conversation. He also liked to present himself in a dramatic light. He once told Osbert and Sacheverell Sitwell that he had lodged in a room that had been occupied by the Ripper, whom he claimed was a veterinary student. Later, in telling the same story to others, he identified the Ripper as a schoolmaster and barrister called Montague Druitt; and later still, if his supposed son is to be believed, Dr Gull. In turn, these representations became part of Sickert's image in the eyes of contemporaries like Max Beerbohm, who noted the charm he held for all women; the two sides of his character, kind and shrewd and then domineering; his cruel mouth and kind eyes.[26]

Yet, the while, Sickert was creating a corpus of work which evolved, not in fits and starts, but with its own centre of gravity and momentum, and in the light of its own internally generated values and conventions. Arguably, he flagged somewhat in his late fifties and early sixties, and seemed to lose his way; but his late sixties saw a resurgence. This coincided with marriage to Lessore and recovery from what seems to have been a stroke, and was sustained well into the next decade. The best of the work he did in his seventies explores and expands upon the qualities already plainly evident in the work he was producing forty-five years earlier, when, as a young man, he was emerging from Whistler's shadow.

In 1932, when he was seventy-two and she forty-one, Sickert wrote a fan letter to the actress Gwen Ffrangcon-Davies and proposed a meeting. He, his wife and Ffrangcon-Davies met for lunch in the restaurant at St Pancras Station. He looked like a 'disreputable old bookmaker', in plaid suit with swallow-tail coat and a grey billycock hat. He drank most of two bottles of champagne, indulged in theatrical reminiscence and succeeded in charming Ffrangcon-Davies completely. They met subsequently, and he found a photograph in her album of press-cuttings from which he painted *La Louve*, a work both monumental – it is more than eight feet tall – and oddly scruffy. 'Terribly Happy and Thrilled the Tate have gone to my Tete', Ffrangcon-Davies telegraphed to Sickert some months later, when *La Louve* had been exhibited and acclaimed, and bought for the nation.[27] It was at this time that Sickert was painting self-portraits, in which he pictured himself, bearded and patriarchal, as Lazarus, as the Servant of Abraham, and then, in the *The Raising of Lazarus*, as Christ. It is this bearded presence, now becalmed, that we see in Cecil Beaton's superb photograph of Sickert and Lessore, taken in 1940, quite soon before Sickert died – perhaps the best photograph of a painter ever taken.

As his fellow painter Frank Auerbach said in introduction to an exhibition of late Sickert, 'Rotten art and great art have something in common: they are both shameless', a quality that, as he grew older, Sickert's work more and more displayed.[28] Always interested in the formulae of picture-making, he not only relied undisguisedly on snapshots and press photographs, but, in some of the oddest of his products – his *Echoes* – produced schematic versions of works which were themselves trivial. Such methods would have been of no interest, as Auerbach remarks, 'if the resulting images had not conjured up grand, living and quirky forms'. But this without question Sickert did. He was not simply a man in the grip of a need to shock or dissimulate. His farouche public posturing served as a safety valve and a defence; and so too, at times, did his painting. Together, his life and work formed a close-knit and gradually evolving system, within which he investigated deep anxieties in a controlled and manageable way.

Considered together, Duras's work and Sickert's have a further implication for the psychology of intimacy. Both explored in a publicly accessible form what others – as children and parents, lovers and spouses – face in private, without the eloquence of pen or brush. It is, perhaps, the exceptional turbulence of their interior lives which prevents artists from keeping the private hidden. On the other hand, it is by reading the works of authors like Duras, by gazing at images like Sickert's, that the rest of us gain insights we would not otherwise gain into our own inner workings. Without such works, the private would remain private: uncharted, occluded.

To an extent not immediately obvious, then, we depend as a culture for our knowledge of the interior life on the feats of people ill-equipped to cope with their private concerns in private. It is they who achieve the vital movement – through the looking glass, from private to public, from fantasy to symbolically significant action – which enables the more conventionally equipped among us to sense what the private *is*.

CHAPTER EIGHT

Parallel Worlds

ART AND INTIMACY ARE separate undertakings, needless to say, and prove for some people mutually antagonistic. Even when inseparably linked, as they are in Duras's novels, the relation between them may prove fraught with paradox. But such caveats aside, our claims about the parallel between the two realms remain substantial. As enterprises, they are psychologically cognate in that they:

Draw on the same imaginative energies;

Create something precious from something mundane;

Afford access to sorts of experience otherwise closed;

Transform individuals' sense of their own capability and range;

Stir deep preoccupations, playing off against one another ideas of the transitory with those of the eternal; and

Evoke an interchangeable language of description and interpretation.

In this chapter, we outline, briefly, a psychological view of the aesthetic response, placing emphasis as we do so on those aspects of recent thinking applicable to intimacy and art alike. The arts, we shall contend, and especially those arts which deal in one way or another with the paradoxes and contradictions of desire, provide the study of intimacy with a royal road. They constitute a world of measurable, analysable images and texts which promise to be useful to the psychologist in much the way that dreams were useful to Freud in his march on the unconscious; valuable both in terms of their content, and of the formal properties they display.

Where, fifty years ago, aesthetics were largely ignored by psychologists, or approached in a mood of philistinism, the psychology of art has of late been revitalised. Certain of its themes illuminate the intimately erotic; and, here, we touch on four. In conclusion, too, we mention an altogether more general feature of thought, of special relevance to an understanding of the arts and of intimate relations, which has tended, recently, to become obscured.

'Feeling into'

In an erotic intimacy that moves us, we gain access to worlds we would previously have regarded as remote or alien. In doing so, we also gain access to previously unenvisaged facets of our own natures. As Matisse remarked, apropos his relation with his model, 'It is by entering into the object that one finds oneself.'[1] If we are to take such paradoxes seriously, and to do their existential significance justice, we have no choice: we must invoke the human capacity for *empathy*.

This notion originated in German nineteenth-century aesthetics, the word being coined in the early years of this century as a translation of the German *Einfühlung*, or 'feeling into'. It is a term which focuses attention on a human attribute easily overlooked because so nearly universal: that of making deep emotional investments in objects which are plainly inanimate. We know that the columns of classical architecture, to take an example, can evoke poignant emotional responses. A column that is proportionally too thin or too fat causes discomfort. As a column rises, we experience the aesthetic equivalent of pain if it swells too much or too little before it tapers; or if its point of maximum swell is too high or too low. We experience the aesthetic equivalent of joy if its swell and taper subtly exceed our expectations yet at the same time reverberate satisfactorily with the other proportions of the façade.

In the same way, we can invest ourselves in paintings and sculptures, and in the characters in plays and novels. By extension, we can also invest ourselves aesthetically in people of flesh and blood. By only the most modest of transpositions, in other words, does the notion of empathy extend from the philosophy of art into the psychology of close relations. There, it is distinguished from the notion of *sympathy*. When we sympathise with others in their misfortunes, we put ourselves in their shoes, temporarily abandoning our objectivity to do this. When we empathise, as Rycroft says, we project ourselves imaginatively into the experience of another person – whether pleasurable or painful – but at the same time retain our sense of ourselves as separate beings.[2]

While eager to enter into worlds of experience other than our own – vicariously, if not in the flesh – we are also sceptical of, and finally unmoved by, any appeal we regard as too flagrant or cheap. As a consequence, empathy exists in a state of tension with its opposite: the 'alienation effect'. A vital role is played both in the management of personal attraction and in the evolution of elicitatory images and texts by the combination of allure with distance. One witnesses this most vividly of all perhaps in jazz. Paul Gonsalves's famous solo in Duke Ellington's 'Diminuendo and Crescendo in Blue' at Newport in 1956 depends for its power to move us – physically, of course, but also more cerebrally – on a species of detachment: a surging and seemingly inexhaustible outpouring of invention allied to a mood recognisably 'cool'.

Pleasurable Surrender

Like any symbolic enterprise, art needs its engine; its instinctually constituted motor. The tendency in the past has been to think of such engines in terms of biological drives like sex, aggression or territoriality that have somehow been diverted or sublimated; but, it now seems widely agreed, this form of analogy is implausibly crude. A more acceptable formulation, discussed in detail in *The Way Men Think*, was offered by Roland Barthes in his last book, *Camera Lucida*.[3] There, with unaccustomed clarity, he writes about the poignancy of still, black-and-white photographs. In doing so, he distinguishes between *studium*, our sensitive appreciation of remarkable things, and *punctum*, the beauty that pierces or impales us. The vast majority of the attentive looking, reading and listening we do qualifies as *studium*; but it is *punctum* that gives art its force. Before certain works, our deliberative intelligence melts away. They puncture the membrane of common sense

98 *Intimate Relations*

with which we protect ourselves from our own fears and desires, and leave us to count the cost.

But how are works of art structured to effect such 'puncturings' – and why is their effect cumulative? Great poems, paintings and pieces of music do not just seize us and release us; we feel moved to return to them, their appeal becoming deeper.

The Management of Ambiguity

Part of an art-work's success or failure as a carrier of poignant emotion lies, we believe, in the use its begetter makes of *ambiguity*. The point is made in extreme form by Hans Bellmer, whose hand-tinted photographs of dolls, produced in the 1930s, remain perhaps the most potently disquieting of all the legacies of surrealism. 'An object', he says, 'a feminine foot for instance, is real only if desire does not take it fatally to be a foot.' It must be seen metaphorically, that is to say, both as a foot and not a foot. Whether as artist or lover, the perceiver's task is to follow the migrations of metaphor in a game devoid of external constraints. The body is 'comparable to a sentence which incites us to disarticulate itself, so that, through an endless series of anagrams, its true contents may be recombined'.[4]

Bellmer's emphasis on the processes of disarticulation and recombination is surely correct. But while ambiguity is essential, it is not boundless. Even within the terms of his chosen parallel, a given sentence permits only a limited set of anagrams; and some will be of more interest than others. In the painstaking construction of his images, and in the evolution of his remarkable personal style, he exploited not random permutations of a doll's body parts, but these parts organised in the light of certain obsessing – some would say, pornographic – themes. Ambiguity thus becomes of aesthetic significance in as much as – consciously or unconsciously – it is *managed*. What is at issue is not difference pursued for its own sake, but:

> The unresolved tension between two complementary but opposed modes of apperception, the recognition of similarity-in-difference and of difference-in-similarity; and

The structuring of emotionally charged thought to which this tension gives rise.[5]

The telling judgements, like those in the detection of differences between the sexes, are typically those of nuance. A famous photograph by Brassai of Matisse and his model captures this well. It shows Matisse as an old man; his model posed before him, as if already part of a typical Matisse image; and, taking shape, the painted image itself.[6] Unstably, the relation between artist and model shifts before the gaze.

Other photographs of Brassai's from the same session are beautiful; and one at least is conceptually complex. But it is to the most famous in the series that one returns. It has a quality of stillness; and, within the bounds created by Brassai's method, it is in this stillness that the conundrums of desire and representation seem most satisfactorily posed.[7]

The psychological states evoked by such arrays can be stable or fluid, of course, and are dependent on form in relation to meaning. The mood of Brassai's photographs of Matisse and his model is conspicuously still: the figures are posed, and the composition encourages the gaze to move slowly and return continually to a state of rest. In contrast, a photographer like Helmut Newton, also influenced by surrealism, contrives a sense of suppressed turbulence. He fashions images that flicker with tension and might almost explode.[8] Analogous effects arise in poetry. In his commentary on John Milton's grand style, Christopher Ricks observes that Milton was a master of 'syntactical fluidity' who achieved 'some of his finest effects precisely by leaving it possible for a word or clause to look backward or forward'. The result, in Empson's words, was 'the sliding, sideways, broadening movement, normal to Milton'; an effect achieved, Ricks shows, not by syntax alone, but by more humble devices like alliteration, punning and word-play.[9]

Asymmetry

The relationship depicted in Brassai's photographs of Matisse and his model is of course asymmetrical. What seems at first sight a

simple relationship turns out to be complex; and as you explore its
complexities, you find not a single symmetrical feature. The image
serves to remind us that all personal relationships of aesthetic significance, from the cradle onwards, have asymmetries at their root.
Asymmetry is the stuff from which both art and amorous fascination are woven.

The artist/model relationship bears in turn on the question of
values. It is sometimes assumed that the parties to an intimacy
have to be the same in all significant respects if they are to be
equals. But what matters in practice, the evidence of art suggests,
is that the relation between the parties is both reciprocal and imaginatively alive. The effort towards sameness, in contrast, cuts the
parties off from just those complex asymmetries and reciprocities
on which the imagination feeds. It is to this perplexing area,
where the psychological and the political are so easily confused,
that we turn in the next chapter.

Containers of Consciousness

Before we do this, there is a point to be made about thought considered in terms of the broadest generality. It is little short of a
truism; but a truism that has recently been obscured as human
scientists struggle among themselves with conventionally scientific
and more radically deconstructive doctrines about how best to ply
their trade.

Even in the most sophisticated circles, there lurks the psychologically naive assumption that a choice must be made between
thought which is artificially constrained or regimented and
thought which is free. Behind this assumption lies another: that
we must choose between the closed and open – between *convergent* systems, within which there are no loose-ends and
worthwhile thought always leads towards greater simplicity; and
divergent systems, in which each attempt at understanding pro-
vokes alternatives, and does so in a proliferation that is in principle
boundless. The first is taken to be symbolic of the hegemony of
mathematics and physical science; while the second plays its part
in the guerrilla war that social scientists and arts specialists fight at
that hegemony's expense.

Yet, in practice, like the detection of similarity and of difference, the convergent and divergent interdepend. Both modes are demanded by the kinds of problem-solving that arise in the everyday practice of mathematics, physical and biological science, technology, the law and medicine; while in the fields of art and of close relations their interplay is manifest and continuous.[10] In both, the most compelling patterns – those which act most successfully as containers of elusive states of consciousness – are typically those in which control is maintained, but is to some degree inconclusive or precarious. It is while in the grip of such deployments of antithetical force that the individual's commitment remains vividly alive:

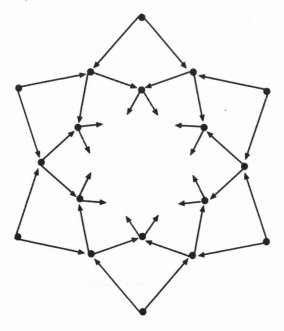

This lattice summarises much of what we have had to say. An emblem, a logo almost, it embodies our central contention: that the imagination is fuelled by thought which is, simultaneously, both disciplined and inconclusive. It is a lattice which 'thinks' metaphorically, by detecting similarities between different elements, and – at one remove – by detecting similarities between those similarities. It links elements to form an array; and while it concentrates attention on that array's centre, it leaves the centre empty.[11]

Such a lattice characterises much of the thinking we do in response both to works of art and to the people who fascinate us.[12] Sometimes, such thinking yields a uniquely satisfactory solution, but more usually it leaves us in doubt: whether because we lack the necessary insight or information, or because, even in principle, a satisfactory solution is not there to be found.[13]

There is not the slightest conceptual difficulty or embarrassment, such lattices remind us, in admitting that:

Works of art and close relations may have important features which are, for all practical purposes, fully determinable, yet defy a complete and satisfactory explanation.

Equally, there is not the least risk of impropriety in acknowledging:

That some readings, whether of works of art or of close relations, may be more veridical than others, in that they more accurately reflect what can and cannot be known about each.

CHAPTER NINE

Issues of Principle:
a Conjecture

THERE REMAINS THE QUESTION of personal values: those issues of principle which, in intimate matters, shape our behaviour. The ground, here, is slippery; the arguments notoriously contentious. Nevertheless, the parallel with the arts remains fruitful. As the Oxford philosopher R. G. Collingwood remarked, 'Art is not indifferent to truth; it is essentially the pursuit of truth.' As he also said, 'Art is knowledge; knowledge of the individual.' Such individual truths and knowledge of them 'become the "terms" between which it is the business of intellect to establish or apprehend relations'.[1] As what holds for art may hold for intimacy, we use this last chapter, therefore, to offer a *conjecture*.

Although our train of thought has its origins in philosophy, biology and the history of art, its aim is to speculate about matters of psychological fact. At heart, the proposition is simple:

That the values which shape our intimate lives are naturally emerging properties of erotic experience itself.

The Basis of Moral Thought

While one cannot easily picture a society worth inhabiting in which impersonal principles (justice, truth), morally loaded maxims ('From each according to his abilities, to each according to his needs'), and value-loaded descriptions (innocent, abusive) play no part, these have been notoriously difficult to justify or apply. Each of the women we have described, from Vera Brittain and Margaret Thatcher to Kate Millett and Gudrun Ensslin, will have seen certain courses of action as just, others as unjust. They would nonetheless have differed violently among themselves about which was which. Philosophy has established no convincing grounds for adjudicating among such judgements; and, as a consequence, it is often assumed that the only defensible policy is to attack whoever or whatever is seen as self-evidently evil or corrupt. If patriarchy or Fascism can once be swept aside, this policy implies, we will each be free. But this approach suffers a weakness as obvious as it is inherent: it can be used not only against male chauvinists and Fascists, but by male chauvinists and Fascists against any group or belief under the sun.

Philosophers like Richard Rorty are insistent on the matter, and we see their insistence as sound. There is no future in hoping against hope, he argues, that there will turn out to be a rational basis for moral judgement or action. David Hume was right. Moral behaviour flows from fellow feeling; and, Rorty believes, it is entirely proper that it should. What is bestial about human relationships, philosophers are now suggesting – not just the pragmatic Rorty, but a thinker with an altogether more Hegelian pedigree like Jean-François Lyotard – occurs when others are seen without sympathy, non-empathically; when the distinctively human capacity for conversation or interlocution is ignored or denied.[2]

This position is minimal, however. In as much as Rorty and Lyotard are positive, they are so in the light of ideas – sympathy, conversation – that they borrow from psychologists and linguists. Their argument can be recast in less apologetic terms if placed squarely within psychology, rather than being allowed to straggle across the no man's land that separates the human sciences from philosophy.

Emergent Properties

When viewed in the context of these recent developments in moral philosophy, Margaret Mead's third husband, Gregory Bateson, may prove to have voiced an insight more trenchant than any of his wife's. In his mature years, Bateson dwelt increasingly on the mind's capacity to organise experience, and he did this less as an anthropologist than a biologist. One of the examples he used is that of binocular vision.[3] The eye's retina 'copies' the visual array before it, passing back this representation to the relevant part of the brain's visual cortex. Although the representations yielded by the two eyes are systematically displaced from one another, the brain reconciles them. In doing so, it achieves something that is present in neither 'copy': namely, depth perception – the ability to read the relative positions of objects in three-dimensional space.

In characterising this feat, Bateson invoked Bertrand Russell's distinction of logical types. Another way of epitomising it is to speak of depth perception as an *emergent property* of the binocular arrangement of the eyes. By analogy, we want to treat intimate values as emergent properties of the needs and fantasies activated by an erotically charged relationship. Some of these values, we believe, are typically the product of a relationship already unfolding; others of a relationship that exists, as yet, only in the imagination. Of the two values we concentrate upon, *equality* seems to belong to the first group, *chastity* to the second.[4]

Artistic Values

Nowhere are beliefs about issues of principle more vehemently voiced than in the artist's studio. It is germane to consider the part played by such beliefs in the life and work of a man like Walter Sickert. For the emotionally charged and visionary ideas he expressed with such conviction plainly arose from within the activity of painting itself, instead of being imported to it from elsewhere.

With characteristic force, Sickert would preach to his pupils Ethel Sands and Nan Hudson about the need to remove all trace of their personal lives and affections from their work. '*Banish your own person, your life and that means you and your affections and yourself from your theatre*', he would insist. '*During the hours you paint*, by using paid models you will forget that you are you and that Nan is Nan and that is *good artistic hygiene* ... There is a constant snare in painting what is part of your life. You cannot avoid with yourself or another artist or a member of your own house or family a spoken or silent dialogue which is *irrelevant* to *light and shade* irrelevant to colour ... I feel so strongly about it ... and I know I am right. The *nullity* and *irrelevance* to yourself of the personality of a model is *tonic*, has *incredible virtues*.'[5]

There is no doubting Sickert's sincerity, or the significance to him of this separation of the artistic from the personal. But what would he have said if either Hudson or Sands had answered back, using as evidence his French contemporaries Pierre Bonnard and Edouard Vuillard, whom he very much admired? Bonnard's nudes expressed undisguisedly his obsession with his wife Marthe, while Vuillard's works arose from the bachelor artist's domestic life with his widowed mother. We cannot know how Sickert would have countered evidence so obviously contrary to his own views, but his position would almost certainly have proved non-negotiable. By one route or another, he would have protected the terrain where he was using the formal concerns of art in managing his more private preoccupations.

Sickert's insistence on the principle of the separation of the personal from the artistic is all the more striking when one considers that, in the earlier parts of his career, he made pencil drawings that closely resemble Bonnard's; and that, later, he fashioned images even a well-versed critic might fail to ascribe correctly to Sickert as opposed to the shy, likeable Vuillard.[6] Yet where Sickert advocated the banishment of the personal, and concentration upon the visual properties of the object, Vuillard had early in his career adopted the belief that the artist should forget the object he was seeking to represent and concentrate instead on that object's 'idea' and 'emotion'.[7] Their points of departure and destination were quite different, as were their rationales for travelling, yet the routes these wholly dissimilar men took lay for appreciable periods of their working lives side by side.[8]

Equality

In as much as the modern love affair or marriage is seen as posing an issue of principle beyond the right to self-fulfilment (or 'self-actualisation'), it is that of equality. The received view is that this is a basic human entitlement, established in the political arena, and transposed from the public to the private. But this line of reasoning is arguably muddled. Individuals of both sexes are now granted political rights, and are (or ought to be) treated equally in all facets of their lives as civic beings. This principle of equality applies evenly to the ownership of matrimonial goods and chat-tels, to the management of a shared household, and the obligations associated with having children. Sometimes, on the other hand, the equality of individuals within an intimacy has a different basis altogether. Far from being a right extended from the realm of home ownership and domestic chores to the sexual, it is a discovery made about the nature of desire itself.

Of primary importance, we argued in Chapter 6, are the frames of mind within which the sexual act occurs: at one extreme, solip-sistic, at the other, conversational. The first is the frame of mind which leads both sexes, and especially perhaps the male, to think of sexual acts in terms of 'scoring'; and which encourages both, especially perhaps the female, to treat the other not as a person but as a conduit. The second is the frame of mind in which, in contrast, the erotic life is no longer the driven coupling of women like Miss Langman and men like P. B. Jones. It becomes, in Lyo-tard's phrase, interlocutory. (To make this distinction is not to assume that the conversational mode is necessarily more real, more mature, more evolved or in any other way inherently superior to the solipsistic; nor that these modes cannot merge, each contain-ing fragments or substrates of the other. It *is* to claim that the conversational mode permits personal discoveries of kinds that the solipsistic mode precludes.)

Under certain conditions, the sexual act allows us to entertain the risks associated with the abandonment and recovery of the deliberative self. When, as John Donne puts it, our waking souls 'watch not one another out of feare', the parties to such an act momentarily cease to be elements in one another's perceptual fields, and are apprehended as sentient beings in their own right.[9] Within each, the boundary separating self from other dissolves; the resulting transformation granting knowledge of another, and altering what we know of ourselves.

Sexual intercourse thus becomes not only a carnal rout but a species of existential inquiry. When certain conditions are met, the sexual act allows us – directly, and without intervening explana-tion – to perceive that the needs and fears of those we desire are of exactly the same order as our own. What the other 'says' at such moments may as a consequence seem of more compelling imagina-tive significance than what we 'say' ourselves. The nature of these enabling conditions is, of course, a matter for factual inquiry. Our own assumption – to put a psychological gloss on Donne – is that sexual intercourse reactivates Oedipal fears; and that the impact of these will vary from couple to couple.

Chastity

In 1634, John Milton completed a masque or pastoral entertainment performed at Ludlow Castle, later known by the name of one of its two central protagonists, Comus.[10] The son of Bacchus and Circe, Comus is a pagan god dedicated to revelry. He waylays travellers and tempts them to drink a magic potion which changes their faces into those of beasts. The potion, it becomes clear, is sexual desire, and the beast-faces are those of individuals in its grasp. A young woman with her two brothers is benighted in a wood; and, separated from them, she meets Comus who leads her off. The brothers follow, and directed by the good Attendant Spirit in the form of a shepherd, find Comus and his rabble pressing their sister, the Lady, against her better judgement to drink the potion. The brothers burst in and put the revellers to flight, but cannot release their sister from the enchanted chair in which she sits; a feat performed by Sabrina, goddess of the neighbouring River Severn, attended by her water nymphs. After an ode of thanks to Sabrina, the Lady and her two brothers return safely to the castle.

Comus was a product of Milton's youth. He was in his mid-twenties at the time; and both the parliamentary revolution and *Paradise Lost* lay well in the future. Even though he saw them as applying to both sexes equally, his themes – chastity, virtue – were ones that Doris Lessing's enlightened and tolerant foursome would have treated as part of the baggage of history: out-of-date and hostile to the human spirit.[11] Margaret Mead would have agreed with them, and there are well-rehearsed arguments which say that she would have been right to do so. There is, nevertheless, another view. Namely, that Mead and Lessing's characters would have been only half-right; that there is a facet to the question which Milton saw and they overlooked. For what *Comus* broaches are the issues of self-deception, especially self-deception when in the grip of sexual desire; and of individuals' rights of sovereignty over their own bodies and minds when in the kinds of predicament that desire creates.

Milton was exploring the quandaries not of rape, that is to say, but of seduction; and was writing not against the fulfilment of desire, but against the capacity of desire to turn us – and turn one another – into beasts, ciphers. Implicitly, he was also calling into question the principle of mutual consent; the assumption that, in states of fear or excitement, we are, each of us, adequately sharpeyed custodians of our own interests. What *Comus* adumbrates – using for the purpose a high-flown rationale that strikes the modern ear quaintly – is the view that the sexual is preeminently a venue for principled action. If it is a function of desire to immobilise our discriminative powers and render us vulnerable to life-warping errors, the solution lies not in the right of individuals to make their own mistakes, but in adherence to a system of values that acts to protect what in hindsight we each cherish most.

When faced with these kinds of quandary, there is nothing so useful, Milton assumes, as good doctrine. Where his theory of chastity is quasi-religious in form, its rationale is as 'problem-solving' or 'action-guiding' as pragmatic philosophers like John Dewey, Charles Sanders Peirce and Rorty could wish. More modern arguments – especially those based on mutual consent – are, in contrast, secular in form but quasi-religious in rationale. The validity of the principles themselves is treated as self-evident, and any challenge to them is made, it is assumed, in bad faith.

Far from being a gratuitous outpouring of high-minded sentiment, *Comus* was commissioned for a particular occasion and had an unusually distressing context. Milton's patron was the Countess of Derby, and her family had recently endured a grotesque sexual scandal, among the most notorious of the era. It concerned the crimes of her son-in-law, the Earl of Castlehaven. Castlehaven had married the Countess of Derby's daughter Anne. Both brought with them children from previous marriages, and one of Anne's children, the twelve-year-old Elizabeth, was married off for dynastic reasons to Castlehaven's eldest son James. Castlehaven is described by one of Milton's biographers as Catholic and homosexual, and as 'plainly mad with perverted lust'.[12] He is said to have had sexual relations with his men servants, and then required them to have intercourse with his wife and to rape his daughter-in-law Elizabeth. There was also the suggestion that Elizabeth

'was used as a whore by the entire household'.[13] His wife, son and
men servants gave evidence against Castlehaven, and he was
executed at Tower Hill in 1631.*

Within a month or two of Castlehaven's execution, however,
the Countess of Derby had a success to celebrate. The husband of
another of her daughters, the Earl of Bridgewater, became president of the Council of Wales, and, soon after, lord lieutenant.
Milton was invited to write a masque of celebration, in which the
children of the family, a fifteen-year-old daughter and her two
younger brothers, could play parts. *Comus* was the result, and it
must have been a delicate exercise; for the Castlehaven scandal
would still have been the subject of prurient gossip, and the family
was pious. As A. N. Wilson points out, Milton's achievement was
not that he wrote a tract against lewdness, but that he wrote
poetry in defence of virtue as the only freedom, and in doing so
gave Comus a share of the best lines.

Most travellers, Milton contends, taste Comus's 'orient liquor'
'through fond intemperate thirst'. Although it changes their
countenances 'into som brutish form', their self-deception is
complete. They:

> Not once perceive their foul disfigurement,
> But boast themselves more comely then before
> And all their friends, and native home forget
> To roule with pleasure in a sensual stie.

Lost in the dark, the Lady finds that 'a thousand fantasies begin to
throng' her memory. She is surrounded by 'calling shapes, and
beckning shadows dire', but reassures herself that such thoughts

---

* Some two miles from us as we write, on the far side of arteries
   ancient and modern – the Grand Union Canal and the M25 motor-
   way – is Harefield Church; there, squeezed in beside the altar, stands
   the Countess of Derby's monument. It takes the form of a brightly
   painted four-poster bed, fashioned by a designer of royal barges and
   stage props called Maximilian Colt. The Countess lies as if asleep,
   'with her golden hair streaming about her, and her coronet on her
   head, her hands together in prayer'; and kneeling beside her at the
   monument's foot are her three daughters.[14] They are similarly carved,
   and can be identified only by their quarterings. One of them is, of
   course, the unfortunate Anne.

need not 'astound the vertuous mind'. When he first sets eyes on the Lady, Comus's response is rhapsodic, and he resolves to make her his queen:

> Can any mortal mixture of Earths mould
> Breath such Divine inchanting ravishment?
> Sure somthing holy lodges in that brest,
> And with these raptures moves the vocal air
> To testifie his hidd'n residence;
> How sweetly did they float upon the wings
> Of silence, through the empty-vaulted night
> At every fall smoothing the Raven doune
> Of darknes till it smil'd . . .

Meanwhile, her elder brother, realising that his sister is lost, voices the danger she faces, and does so in terms of the conflict between chastity and desire:

> So dear to Heav'n is Saintly chastity,
> That when a soul is found sincerely so,
> A thousand liveried Angels lacky her,
> Driving far off each thing of sin and guilt,
> And in cleer dream, and solemn vision
> Tell her of things that no gross ear can hear . . .

As a consequence, the 'unpolluted temple of the mind', is turned 'by degrees to the souls essence'. Lust, on the other hand:

> By unchaste looks, loose gestures, and foul talk,
> But most by leud and lavish act of sin,
> Lets in defilement to the inward parts,
> The soul grows clotted by contagion,
> Imbodies, and imbrutes, till she quite loose
> The divine property of her first being.

When Comus places the Lady in an enchanted chair, and offers her the glass, she refuses to drink and moves to rise, but finds that she cannot. Comus, confident in his power over her, coaxes her to see pleasure as innocent:

> Why are you vext Lady? why do you frown?
> . . . Why should you be so cruel to your self,
> And to those dainty limms which nature lent
> For gentle usage, and soft delicacy?

But the Lady is adamant:

> Thou has nor Ear, nor Soul to apprehend
> The sublime notion, and high mystery
> That must be utter'd to unfold the sage
> And serious doctrine of Virginity.

Comus seems to sense danger – 'a cold shuddring dew dips me all o're' – but still rejects her views as 'meer moral babble', and prepares to press his case with more vigour:

> . . . one sip of this
> Will bathe the drooping spirits in delight
> Beyond the bliss of dreams. Be wise, and taste . . .

At this point the brothers rush in, and although she has still to be released from the chair which immobilises her, the Lady's temptation is over.

The values *Comus* expresses are easily seen as priggish, but Milton was not a prig in the sense that we would nowadays understand the term. 'He is often spoken about', Wilson observes, 'as humourless, dour, and sombre, where it would be more appropriate to think of him as shrill, fantastical, and malicious.'[15] He wrote eloquently in defence of divorce and of the freedom of the press. He was sociable, at times remarkably generous, and possessed good looks about which he was vain. A scornful and vituperative controversialist, his work at such times shows 'a marked contrast between the concentrated, almost awed seriousness with which he talks about himself', and his ruthlessness in ridding himself of his enemies, quite gratuitously accusing one of copulating in garden-sheds.[16]

Milton fell in love more than once, and married three times, but an air of mystery hangs about him, especially his first marriage. He married Mary Powell when he was thirty-four and she sixteen or seventeen. After a few weeks, she left him and went back to live with her Royalist parents in the country outside Oxford; and it was three years before she came back. Soon after her return she became pregnant; and some months later, her whole unruly family arrived in her train as refugees of the Civil War. She died in childbirth in 1652, the year in which Milton became blind, leaving him with three daughters, with whom, in later life, his relationships were poor. He remarried, but his second wife Catherine Wood-cock died less than two years later, again as a consequence of childbirth. In 1662, he married Elizabeth Minshull and she sur-vived him.

It seems that Milton had fallen in love at least once before meet-ing Mary – with a girl called Emily or Emilia who was perhaps Italian and whom he met when he was twenty.[17] She elicited from him five sonnets and a canzone; but nothing came of it. He may have fallen in love with Mary too, although authorities are here divided. He certainly married her within weeks of their first meet-ing. Some see it as a love-match, on his part at least, but as imprudent; others as expedient. John Broadbent, alluding to Mil-ton's views on divorce, speaks of him as 'chained to a carcase' and as 'gripped with horrified despair'.[18] On the other hand, Milton would seem to have loved his second wife Catherine with suffi-cient intensity to write for her one of the most eloquent of all statements of bereavement: the sonnet that begins, 'Methought I saw my late espoused Saint/Brought to me like *Alcestis* from the grave . . .' , and ends, 'But O as to embrace me she enclin'd/I wak'd, she fled, and day brought back my night.' What passed be-tween Milton and his late espoused saint we do not know; but, within the framework of his own beliefs, it could have included intense sexual pleasure for both, as long as this served the 'souls essence', rather than being 'leud and lavish'. Desire might have suffused their imaginations precisely because their sexual exchanges were associated with 'sublime notions' and 'high mysteries'.

Milton was a devout Christian and was fascinated by Christian-ity, but 'by Luther's standards, or Calvin's, or Zwingli's, or Cranmer's', Wilson observes, he 'was probably not a Christian at all'.[19] In his *De Doctrina Christiana*, the fruit of years of pains-taking theological deliberation, Milton endorses the Protestant view of the individual as relating directly to God, rather than through the mediation of priests and bishops, and as doing so without regard to dogma. Dispensing with orthodoxy, he was driven to evolve a theology of his own, and many of the con-clusions he reached have subsequently been seen as heretical. He argued against the Trinity, against Christ's divinity, and against the notion of God creating all things, visible and invisible out of nothing. More startlingly, he appeared to advocate polygamy.

Milton had instinctive contempt for the convention-bound and institutional. He conceived of human beings as free; but he remained a traditionalist in that he saw this freedom as constrained by the need for salvation: the requirement that, in the end, we must each meet a dispassionately appraising eye and be judged. In his own case, this meant presenting himself for judgement with each lurch of the libido – for the beautiful Emilia, for Mary Powell, for Catherine Woodcock whom he could feel but not see, even for a certain Miss Davis – arranged not with the past tidied away behind the present, but side by side, and in an unwavering light.

Comus is a product of youthful energy, not painfully acquired experience. Broadbent, who is sceptical of this phase in Milton's poetic development, speaks of him as 'rationalising into a pseudo-Platonic doctrine of chastity what were really three aspects of the same complex, his shyness, his lust, and his cosmographical ambition'.[20] Wilson, on the other hand, sees *Comus* as expressing beliefs that were to remain Milton's throughout his life: in particular his faith in virtue as freedom's necessary and sufficient condition. We see Broadbent's view as having the ring of psychological truth, but nevertheless sense in *Comus* a truth of another kind. What separates us from the beasts, Milton's argument suggests, is neither language nor culture, but the capacity to shape our desires in the light of principle.

Desires and Inducements

If Milton was wrong about the power of religious or quasi-religious doctrine to shape the sexual experience of the young, he was right to see the sharpest conflicts as those of temptation. At issue are not inducements to do what we find repugnant; rather, inducements that play on our divided natures, encouraging us to override scruples and explore facets of experience previously denied or held in check.

The issue is spelt out by Steven Marcus in his commentary on *My Secret Life*. The author of these eleven volumes, a man of social position and at times wealth, was hugely promiscuous, and his appetites became more experimental as he grew older. His standard procedure was to pay poor women to have intercourse with him. In time, more than a thousand succumbed, and he conveys the impression that most did so gladly, appreciative of the money and the sex too. Like Comus, he sees sex as 'the great humanizer of the world'; sex and democracy somehow becoming equated in his mind.[21]

The sentiment is a charming one, as Marcus says, but as *My Secret Life* itself liberally demonstrates, it happens not to be true. The effect on the author of his sexual obsession is anything but humanising. While sex fascinates him, so does its relation to money. Not only does he keep careful accounts of what his sexual encounters cost; on two occasions he attempts to fill a woman's vagina with shilling pieces to see how many it will contain. 'It is not only in political revolutions that crimes are committed in the name of liberty.'[22]

On one occasion, the author of *My Secret Life* describes himself as walking in the London mist and noticing on the opposite side of the road two girls singing, laughing and talking loudly as they walk. As a man carrying a basket on his back passes them, he makes an indecent suggestion. 'Tickle us up then', replies one, loudly, before both run off laughing, evidently having enjoyed the bawdy exchange. The author follows them, falls into conversation, and is soon offering cash for favours. 'Give me a kiss and I will give each of you sixpence', the author records himself as saying. While kissing the larger of the two, he whispers 'I'll give you a shilling if you will do something for me and get your companion away.' She gets rid of her friend, comes back, but is embarrassed. 'You old beast', she says, 'let me go'; but having broken away does not go far. They make arrangements to meet again, and the pattern repeats itself, he buying from her sexual contacts of a preliminary kind, she partly acquiescent, partly prevaricating. She returns, he eventually realises, when she has spent the money he has given her 'in fruit, sugar candy and bull's eyes, and in riding in omnibuses'.

Their exchanges reach a crisis when he gets her into a cab and, determined to have intercourse with her, offers her a sovereign, advising that she can wrap it in a piece of paper, make it muddy, and tell her mother that she found it. 'The girl was silent long, looking me in the face (as it seemed) in the dark.' She is going to yield, he senses; and, unasked, she once more places her hand on his member. If she won't submit, he tells her, he won't see her again; he can get fifty girls to do what she is doing for a shilling. Has any other girl done it, she asks. When he tells her that a dozen have, the response is 'Lor', and she seems to reflect on the information he has given.[23] Eventually he tries to force her; she cries out and fights back. As they struggle he ejaculates without succeeding in entering her; and there his venture ends. She gets out of the carriage, runs off, is lost in the darkness, and he never sees her again.

In such cases of near-rape, as Marcus points out, two possibilities, or roles, are at war in the mind of the woman. 'On the one side, she wants to assert her existence as a human being with absolute rights over her own person. On the other, money, brute force, a *fait accompli*, and the cumulative power of a whole social system press her toward resignation.'[24] The issues are more subtle, but no less those of principle, when, as happens here, the girl in question is plainly intrigued, whether for mercenary reasons or sexual reasons, but finally draws back. Afterwards, the author commits to the page his astonishment that 'I should have taken all that trouble for a dirty little working girl, whose face I never saw excepting by the light of a street lamp.' He reflects, too, that 'it is not gentlemen who get the virginities of these poor little bitches, but the street boys of their own class'. Finally, however, his attitude is sanguine. At a cost of a pound or two, this undertaking has amused him, as all chance adventures do, breaking 'the monotony of matter of fact hard fucking'.[25]

What this girl is defending, Marcus insists, is not just her body but her self-respect. 'When we see this young girl resisting all that money, class, privilege, and power', he says, 'we understand how vital an importance the moral idea of respectability could have for persons in her circumstances. Even more, a work like *My Secret Life* leads one to understand how the deflection of one's sexuality, how even frigidity itself, could have an important social function or purpose.'[26] Locked together, wrestling in the back of that cab while the driver turned a deaf ear, the girl was battling for something precious: her freedom not to do what she intuits is wrong. Why she should in the end have thwarted the man, we do not know; but baulk she does, and most of us applaud. Perhaps the subliminal messages the man conveyed as he moved from persuasion to force changed. Like Comus, he may have felt a cold shuddring dew that dipped him all o're.

The implication, from the point of view of our own argument, is that the phenomena of attempted seduction and near-rape force us to distinguish closely between just those issues of principle that are glossed over or denied in talk about sex as a vehicle for self-fulfilment. To put the point negatively, it is simply not the case that most people would view as interchangeable the four courses of action open to this girl: that she has intercourse with the author and takes his sovereign, that she accepts the intercourse but rejects the sovereign, that she takes the sovereign but avoids intercourse, or – as happened – takes flight and leaves the sovereign behind. Nor is it the case that we can resolve the uncertainty such an episode creates by asking whether the relationship in question is 'abusive'. Her relationship with the man may be entirely friendly, yet it may still be advisable for the girl to say (and mean) 'No': because it felt wrong, because she would later regret giving way, or because it would compromise what chance she had of a fruitful and self-respecting future.

It is possible to see both the man's lechery and the girl's reluctance in the face of temptation as the product of a repressive society, shot through with 'Victorian' values; a simple view, rehearsed at length in the course of the last thirty years or so. Marcus looks closer, however. He concludes 'that in the degree to which that young girl succeeded in denying her sexuality to the author, and to other men, and in the degree to which she even made her own sexuality inaccessible to herself, in that degree might she have the chance of extending her humanity in other directions.'[27]

The human mind – as Freud insisted – is characteristically a system which represses part of its activity in response to its own internally generated anxiety; not one that displays anxiety or aberration because parts of its activity are externally repressed. On this argument, a preoccupation with self-respect, implicitly defined in sexual terms, forms a natural part of a girl's ruminations from an early age. If our own conjecture is correct, it is from the childish glimmerings Marcus adumbrates that there emerges the possibility of principled thought about our intimate lives as adults. It may also be true that the capacity to sustain an erotic intimacy depends on the energy inherent in the tension between such principled thought and the fantasies generated by the requirements of the flesh.

Notes

Introduction

1. *The Way Men Think* evoked an interesting response. Faced with a text about the psychology of men, many readers reacted by talking insistently – at times unstoppably – about women. As our culture at present stands, it seems that maleness is what is left over when you have exhausted the topic of women.

1: Allowing the Clockwork to Run

1. See, particularly, Greenson (1968), Stoller (1974) and Chodorow (1978). Although indebted to psychoanalysis, we see human development as reconciling the effects of three different kinds of cause – the biological, the cultural and the intra-psychic – and we make no assumption about the priority in a particular context of one over another.
2. The notion of identifying oneself with another person is ambiguous. It can mean much the same as 'model oneself upon' or 'imitate'. It can also mean 'put yourself in the shoes of'. We do our best to restrict our use of 'identify' to the first of these usages.
3. Like most theoretical constructs inside science or out, the developmental patterns and frames of mind described here are heuristic devices, explanatory fictions. They serve a function analogous to that of a designer's sketch.
4. Hegel's notion of self-estrangement (*Selbstentfremdung*) was the antecedent of more recent preoccupations with alienation and otherness – e.g., Marx's and Brecht's. Hegel saw self-estrangement as central to man's growing self-consciousness, and as such it was a development of which he approved. Later, Marx used three notions all of which have been translated as 'alienation': *Vergegenständlichung*, or objectification, which means roughly the same as the Anglo-Saxon philosopher's 'reification'; *Entfremdung*, or 'estrangement'; and *Entäusserung*, or the sale of oneself as a commodity. Some child psychologists (see, e.g., Trevarthen and Logotheti 1989) have recently argued that the duality between 'self' and 'other' is innate; and that it provides the format within which actual encounters with others are contained.
5. Closely adjacent to the idea of living-in-relation is that of the 'relational self': the vision of human beings as creatures whose primary developmental requirement is to establish personal bonds, and who create from

within the framework of these bonds a performance of themselves that is authentically their own (Jack 1991). Influential in this respect have been Bowlby's (1988) theorising about attachment, and Stern's (1985) observational studies of developing infants. Just as the traditional view of the self, based on the ideas of separation and individuation, epitomises the developmental requirements of the male, so that of the relational self epitomises those of the female. The position is at present confused by the tendency to treat the relational self as normal or natural, and the individuated self as aberrant. An antidote is to be found in the often-repeated observation (see, e.g., Roe 1953, Storr 1988, Hudson and Jacot 1991) that there are men who have highly creative lives in which personal relationships play little or no part. Whether there are women who are similarly placed remains to be established.

6. Jack, op. cit. In a field like musical composition, until recently dominated by men but now being colonised by women, certain gifts may turn out to be sex-linked. Women may compose in ways that are perceived by both sexes as aesthetically significant, but as lacking certain distinctively 'male' characteristics: a commitment, say, to formal rigour or the ability to write tunes which ravish.

7. Keller (1985).

8. Hodgkin (1988). For the last thirty years, it has been fashionable for theorists of knowledge to dismiss out of hand the possibility that, in themselves, facts could ever constitute a foundation for what we know (Kuhn 1962). An irony of this extreme view is that while it is assumed to liberate the oppressed (and particularly women) from tyranny, it obscures the quality of dispassion that may prove to be among women's most telling intellectual advantages.

   For those interested in etymology, it is worth noting that in the sixteenth century 'fact' meant an evil deed or crime, a sense which now lingers in the phrases 'before the fact' and 'after the fact' (Ricks 1963). Perhaps it is not entirely fanciful to see it lingering, too, in the minds of those philosophers and sociologists committed to cleanse knowledge rather than elucidate it.

9. Gilligan (1982), p.42.

10. Jack, p.221. As Eichenbaum and Orbach (1994) say, expressing the daughter's position *vis-à-vis* the mother, 'We are merged with her and have no sense of where we begin or where she ends' (p.29). The notion that distinctive themes characterise psychological development in girls is clearly articulated by Zilbach (1993).

    Not discussed in our text are the complex phenomena of the mother's identification with her son: the tendency of some mothers to primp and feminise their sons; the tendency of others to empathise with their sons in their conventionally masculine accomplishments.

11. The historical development of psychoanalytic thinking about sex differences has recently been reviewed by Breen (1993). The notions of mother/daughter rivalry and of the infant's ambivalence towards the mother are of course essential features not only of the Oedipus Complex as classically conceived, but of more recent formulations, Freudian and Kleinian alike. What is distinctive in our claim about the female incubus is that we see the ambivalences of the small girl towards her mother as

remaining unresolved in the normal as well as the neurotic case; and as doing so because there are no formal arrangements internal to the female psyche which might act to resolve them. These ambivalences are of a kind which can be resolved partially rather than completely, and in adulthood rather than infancy or childhood.

12. Radloff (1980), Weissman (1987).
13. Diagrams of this kind provide only a rough-and-ready mapping of one layer onto the next. So there will be an untidy association between reproductive anatomy and object choice; and, likewise, between either of these and the frames of mind we characterise here as typically 'female' and typically 'male'.

The use of geometry in modelling psychological states and processes is touched on in Hudson (1975). Readers interested in the geometry itself will find Critchlow (1969) rewarding. Those with an appetite for a mathematically sophisticated application of geometry to the modelling of behaviour will find it in Abraham and Shaw (1988).

14. Recently, Estela Welldon (1991) has argued persuasively that while both sexes are capable of perversion, they differ in the forms their perversity takes. In men, she believes, such activity is aimed outside themselves; in women, against themselves – either against their own bodies or against their children. Our own view remains, nonetheless, that where a perversion like fetishism occurs in a female, it does so as part of a disturbance of gender identity (Hopkins 1984); and that, for reasons associated with the male wound, such perversions will remain numerically dominated to an overwhelmingly extent by males (Hudson and Jacot 1991, p.126).

At present, the tendency among psychoanalytical theorists is to consider perversion in terms of object relations theory. In a thoughtful paper, on the other hand, Redfearn (1982) has urged that a clear distinction be maintained between the part-object/whole-object dimension and the thing/person dimension. Our impression is that not two but three pairs of categories are currently confused: part-object/whole-object, person/thing, self/other.

2: A Thought Experiment: Public and Private Lives

1. Thought experiments are familiar among theoretical physicists and philosophers (Sorensen 1992); and, as has recently been pointed out, they play a part in the ethnomethodological tradition of sociology developed by Garfinkel (Place 1992). They also arise at the confluence of psychology and linguistics; Johnson-Laird and Oatley's (1989) use of the 'but' test to decide whether two words are semantically related constituting a thought experiment of sorts. On the other hand, surprisingly little use has been made of thought experiments in mainstream psychology, especially in probing what particular bodies of evidence mean.
2. Like Margaret Thatcher but five years her junior, Shirley Williams was a student at Somerville College, Oxford. Having graduated, she worked as a journalist, as her mother had. She entered parliament and became secretary of state for education and science in the Labour government

swept from office by Thatcher's victory in 1979. She married Bernard Williams, a philosopher, but subsequently divorced him. Like her father George Catlin, she later became a professor of politics at a North American university – in his case, Cornell; in hers, Harvard.

3. Bailey (1987), p.83.
4. Leishman and Spender (1952), p.11. In Rilke, the mood quite quickly passed, leaving him depressed.
5. Bailey, p.13.
6. Catlin travelled widely, and was active in the international politics of the moderate left. He worked for the Fabian Society, and was joint founder of the English-Speaking Union. Twice he stood unsuccessfully for parliament as a Labour MP; and was eventually knighted in 1970, the year Vera died.

   The relationship between Brittain and Holtby is often thought to have been lesbian, but, Bailey says, there is no evidence that this was so. On the other hand, Brittain's sense of decorum in intimate matters ran deep.
7. Millett (1970). Millett's attitude towards the family echoes that of Karl Marx and Friedrich Engels, a century before. The modern family, Marx claimed, 'contains *in miniature* all the contradictions which later extend throughout society': Engels (1942), p.60. Marx and Engels had in turn been influenced by the American anthropologist Lewis Morgan; like James Frazer, an apostle of society's capacity for evolutionary change.
8. Millett (1991). On the strength of her royalties from *Sexual Politics*, and the funds her success brought her, Millett and Kerr established a community for women at a farm in Poughkeepsie.
9. Ibid., p.127.
10. Ibid., p.18.
11. Ibid., p.128.
12. Ibid., p.129.
13. Ibid., p.130.
14. Ibid., p.133.
15. Margaret Thatcher is a figure whom many psychologists and social scientists ignore – because, it is said, she is so obviously a surrogate man (see, e.g., Morgan 1989). Our own impression, on the contrary, is that she has been ignored because her political beliefs are conservative, and because her presentation of self is conventionally feminine. Her career also highlights a difficulty more specifically American. It is in the United States that feminism has taken its most outspoken forms; but America, conspicuously, is a country in which women do not rise to power. Both relatively progressive countries like Norway and relatively hidebound ones like the United Kingdom and France have produced female prime ministers. So too have India, Pakistan, Sri Lanka, the Philippines, Israel, Turkey.
16. Junor (1983), p.1.
17. Ibid., p.2.
18. Young (1989), p.5. Young's is, from the psychologist's point of view, a model biography; and we draw on it heavily in what follows.
19. Ibid., p.4.
20. Rycroft (1985).

21. Young, p.16.
22. Ibid., p.38.
23. Ibid., p. 34. Her legal training may also have alerted Mrs Thatcher to the way in which the law could be used as a vehicle of political change. She was, Young claims, the first prime minister of the modern, statute-bound political era in a position to do so. On the other hand, it was partly her unbending commitment to a fiscal innovation, the Poll Tax, which was eventually her undoing.
24. Ibid., p.38.
25. Junor, p.41.
26. Ibid., p.305.
27. Grove (1992).
28. Junor, p.40.
29. Ibid., p.43.
30. Ibid., p.140.
31. Like politicians, civil servants execute positioning manoeuvres as if by instinct. Robert Armstrong's career appeared to be blighted when Mrs Thatcher became prime minister. He had been Edward Heath's private secretary, and Heath was the politician whose very life-work Mrs Thatcher existed to repudiate. As soon as she became leader of the opposition, however, Armstrong arranged a meeting with Mrs Thatcher, with the aim of ensuring that his face was familiar to her. 'Mrs Thatcher's staff at the time noted with amusement', Young observes, 'the determination he showed in contriving the encounter' (p.163).
32. Young, p.164. The same rule governed Thatcher's appointment of women; for example that of her secretary Alison Ward (Junor, p.74).
33. Young, p.165.
34. Junor, p.118.
35. Ibid., p.164.
36. Our copy of *One of Us*, bought secondhand, is inscribed 'Christmas 89/90. dear heart – Your pin-up girl revealed as never before! Happy reading (when I'm not around). Julie XX.'
37. For those who scan their political leaders' public performances for reassuring signs of mental health, Mrs Thatcher was to cause the occasional tremor – as, for example, when she took to referring to herself in public as 'we'. Post and Robins (1993) examine the problems posed when political leaders fall ill while in office.

3: The Thought Experiment Continued: Telling the Truth

1. By the time she was an adolescent, Margaret Mead was later to estimate, perhaps fancifully, she had lived in sixty homes and eaten food prepared by 107 cooks.
2. Howard (1984), p.22. Howard's biography provides excellent coverage, especially of the more personal aspects of Mead's life.
3. Lola Romanucci-Ross, quoted by Freeman (1991), p.123.
4. Howard, p.392.
5. Mead (1969), p.129.

6. Howard, p.25.
7. Ibid., p.44.
8. Ibid., p.295.
9. Ibid., p.357.
10. Ibid., p.253.
11. Ibid., p.406.
12. Ibid., p.363.
13. Ibid., p.111.
14. Ibid., p.253.
15. Ibid., p.49.
16. Ibid., p.253.
17. Ibid., p.258. Gregory Bateson's father, a 'virulent and extraverted' man, invented the science of genetics, and named his son after Gregor Mendel. He inspired in Gregory both fear and fascination; the one time he remembered touching his father 'was wiping his nose after he died' (Lipset 1978, p.28). Gregory Bateson was original and of a systematic turn of mind (Bateson 1972, 1979). It was he, for instance, who first formulated the notion of the double-bind. He makes an important contribution to our own argument in Chapter 9.
18. Howard, p.258.
19. Ibid., p.217. She breast-fed her daughter as she herself had been, but subsequently played little part in her daughter's physical care.
20. The claims Mead made in *Sex and Temperament* (1935) on the basis of their New Guinea research were momentous. Our sex roles, she concluded, could be put on and taken off as easily as our clothes. Fortune subsequently published an article contradicting his wife (Fortune 1939), but thereafter his protests were restricted to a narrowly professional circle. He held back, his niece and executor Ann McLean believed, partly from distaste at laundering dirty linen in public, partly because he realised how futile it would be to take on the press (Howard, p.163).
21. Writing home in 1913, Rupert Brooke had said, 'If you ever miss me, suddenly . . . you'll know that I've got sick for the full moon on those little thatched roofs, and the palms against the morning, and the Samoan boys and girls diving thirty feet into a green sea or a deep mountain pool – and that I've gone back' (quoted in Howard, p.77).
22. There ensued gatherings of American anthropologists in which Freeman was denounced, and articles were published in which his good faith and technical competence were impugned. As with psychologists in the context of the Cyril Burt scandal, his critics faced a grave challenge. At issue was the good name of their discipline; and, dependent on that good name, the flow of funds, posts and talented students on which the vitality of any academic enterprise depends.
23. Freeman (1991), p.104. In this article, Freeman documents Mead's Samoan fieldwork, and also gives access by means of references and commentary to the debate his criticisms provoked.
24. Ibid., p.114.
25. Mead (1969), p.83.
26. Freeman, p.109.
27. Howard, p.75.

28. Freeman, p.109.
29. It has recently been argued (Kuper 1989) that the anthropologist's task is more subtle than had previously been imagined. The implication is that anthropology is less akin to natural history, more to the translation of poetry from one language to another. If so, anthropology's neighbours should be alerted. They need to know whether they are dealing with an enterprise adjacent to the more factual branches of sociology, or one abutting literary criticism and Gallic philosophy.
30. Howard, p.321.
31. We are indebted to Prof. Freeman for making available to us a copy of the abstract of Margaret Mead's master's essay. Her topic, suggested to her by Boas, was at first sight a routine exercise in intelligence testing. But it was in fact designed to illuminate an issue then preoccupying Boas: the relation of nature to nurture – and, implicitly, of the biological sciences to the social ones. Following in her mother's footsteps, Mead gave intelligence tests to 276 Italian immigrant and 160 American children. She showed not only that the Italian children stood to a disadvantage, but that the extent of this disadvantage depended on the amount of English that the Italian children's parents spoke in the family home. It was a well-conceived piece of work; and gave Mead the opportunity she would always relish: to improve a climate of opinion, 'to build a better world'. It also enabled her to display both technical competence and a formidable capacity for hard work. You cannot help wondering, nevertheless, whether her master's research was all it seemed. The possibility remains that here, too, she cut corners and filled gaps, perhaps inventing whole swathes of data, or dressing them up after the event.
32. Freeman, p.112.
33. It remains unclear to what extent Mead was committed to the Boasian point of view. Throughout her career she sought out the company of psychologists and psychoanalysts, seemed to see herself as a 'spoilt psychologist', and was a firm advocate of psychoanalysis for everyone except herself. She also remained interested in some of psychology's more obviously biological branches; somatotyping, for instance, in which the personality is linked to body type.

    Late in life, she contributed to a collection of essays in honour of Bateson (Brockman 1978). In this she combines disparate sets of observations in a way that remains startlingly fresh: on non-reciprocity among East European Jews, on the spectator in French culture, and on male dominance in Thai culture. She rounds off her contribution with a tabulation of the systematic sex differences displayed in the seven Pacific Island cultures she had studied. 'Whether these universals were to be attributed to biological sex differences', she says, 'or to the elaboration of the experiential circumstance that women bore and reared children, was and is not yet clear' (ibid., p.222). In her seventies, plainly, her attitudes were far from those of a naive or dogmatic environmentalist. They might even have passed muster in a department of ethology or animal behaviour.
34. Israels and Schatzman (1993), p.26.
35. Ibid., p.47. Freud's sample initially numbered thirteen cases (Standard

Edition, 3, p.164); and was subsequently increased to eighteen (SE, 3, p.207). The confusion over the identity of the assailants is pointed out in the Standard Edition in editorial footnotes. Freud's first clearly and publicly disavowed actual seduction in favour of unconscious fantasy in his paper 'My Views on the Part Played by Sexuality in the Aetiology of the Neuroses' (SE, 7, p.274), written in 1905 and published in Loewenfeld's book *Sexualleben und Nervenleiden* in 1906.

36. The years 1896 and 1897 – he was then entering his forties – were a time of crisis for Freud. Within a period of little more than a year, his father had died, he had ceased to have sexual relations with his wife, he had undertaken his self-analysis, and the possibility of a medical scandal – Fliess's bungled operation on 'Irma's' nose – was preying on his mind.

As a letter he wrote to Karl Abraham in 1924 shows, he also came to see psychoanalysis and laboratory science as separate worlds. 'It is making severe demands on the unity of the personality', he claimed, 'to try and make me identify myself with the author of the paper on the spinal ganglia of the petromyzon. Nevertheless I must be he, and I think I was happier about that discovery than about others since' (Sulloway 1979, p.2). The possibility must be that, in leaving laboratory science, Freud saw himself as entering a world of theory in which facts could be used to serve, in effect, as window-dressing. Whatever the precise explanation, it appears that:

By 1896, in certain contexts at least, Freud was treating facts as essentially decorative;

As early as 1896 or 1897, his attitude towards the identity of his patients' seducers was ambivalent or confused; and

Well into old age, he remained confused both about whether the victims' recollections were consciously accessible or repressed and accessible only through interpretation.

To an extent not previously acknowledged, in other words, Freud qualifies as one of history's great 'sleepwalkers' (Koestler 1959). Like Kepler, he reached the truth – if that is what the Oedipus Complex is – in spite of profound and persisting confusion.

37. Freud's analysis of Anna seems to have begun in 1918 and to have lasted into the early 1920s, Roazen (1970) being the first to make this alarming episode public. Young-Bruehl (1989) produces persuasive circumstantial evidence that a central part in Anna's analysis was played by her sexual fantasies of beating; although whether these were based on actual beatings by her father is unclear.

38. Freeman, p.118. Our view of Mead's character and motives may prove to differ sharply from that of Prof. Freeman: see his forthcoming book *The Fateful Hoaxing of Margaret Mead*.

39. As recently as the 1960s, human scientists were expected to distinguish clearly between 'theory' and 'the facts', theory ceasing to be purely hypothetical only to the extent that factual evidence underpins it – an assumption that reigns to this day in, for example, medical research. Critics like Kuhn (1962) have argued, on the contrary, that facts are always contained within, and subservient to, the paradigm or perspective of the person who seeks them out, assesses their relevance and

brings them to bear. But while offered as a liberation, this relativistic view has in turn become oppressive, being the instrument with which those who control disciplines like sociology and anthropology marginalise the unorthodox and stifle evidence of incompetence or fraud.

What is needed, it seems to us, is the best of both worlds. Certainly, no view of the human sciences is worth promoting unless it (a) helps sharpen the scrutiny of research which is confused or dishonest; and (b) creates space within which research, however brilliant its inspiration or method, can be shown to be mistaken.

40. Freeman, p.119.
41. Ibid., p.119. Associated with the temptations of high-handedness there lurks another. It concerns factual claims which are startling or over-inconclusive. Freud, it seems, displayed just this frailty. As Josef Breuer observed, he was 'given to absolute and exclusive formulations'; a habit which was expressive, Breuer believed, of a 'psychical need' (Schatzman 1992). Typically, such pseudo-factual claims are made forcefully and to audiences, rather than cautiously and in private; and, at first sight, their purpose is polemical. But observation suggests a more interesting motive: that they take the over-emphatic and factual form they do in order to overcome an inhibition. They are thrust across the threshold separating private from public rather as parents thrust shy children.

4: At Close Quarters

1. Bailey (1987), p.81.
2. Becker (1989). Becker gives valuable biographical information about the members of the Red Army Faction, especially Ulrike Meinhof.
3. Ibid., p.53.
4. Ibid., p.55.
5. Ibid., p.58. Andreas Baader was born in 1943, the son of a historian and archivist killed on the Russian front in 1945; and was brought up by his mother and female relatives, all of whom doted on him. Described by Becker as 'very pretty indeed, with long black eyelashes and blue mischievous eyes', he grew up to be sulky, lazy and 'immune to all kinds of scruple'. As a young adult, he was attractive to women, and he swaggered. Prior to meeting Ensslin and undertaking his career as a terrorist, he seems scarcely to have worked, living with (and off) a gregarious and easy-going action painter called Ellinor Michel.
6. Ibid., p.70.
7. Ibid., p.55.
8. Ibid., p.70.
9. Ibid., p.82.
10. Ibid., p.218.
11. Ibid., p.228.
12. MacDonald (1991). Morgan (1989) claims of Meinhof and Ensslin that 'whether as troops or as "leaders", these women were followers. Their "rebellion" for love's sake is classic feminine – not feminist – behavior' (p.208). This seems far-fetched, especially as applied to Ensslin. About Ronconi, an interesting case from the feminist point of view, Morgan says nothing.

13. MacDonald, p.189.
14. Ibid., p.194.
15. Marcuse (1969), p.20.
16. Tillich (1974), p.203.
17. Becker, p.208.
18. Ibid., p.44.
19. Ibid., p.29.
20. Hite (1988).
21. Ibid., p.804 and following.
22. Barham (1994). Ms Barham is described as writing for BBC Radio and *Spitting Image*, and as being a past winner of the BBC/Witzend TV scriptwriting competition.
23. *Marriage and Divorce Statistics, 1991* (1993).
24. Festy (1985). See also *Marriage and Divorce Statistics, 1837–1983* (1990). Changes in legislation obviously exert an influence over marriage and divorce statistics, but their impact is by no means straightforward, tending to follow change as much as to promote it. The impact of institutionalised religion is likewise complex. Rates of divorce per 100 marriages in Protestant Norway and Catholic France, for example, have echoed one another quite closely in the period between 1935 and 1981, as have those in the Netherlands and Belgium.

    The calculation of rates of divorce per 100 marriages is a useful index, but it introduces a time-lag of a decade or more; and this becomes confounded, in the short-term at least, with other changes – for example, those in the age at which people first marry. Such effects can be both rapid and sizeable. In England and Wales, the average age at first marriage increased by more than two years in the decade between 1981 and 1991, the averages in 1991 standing at 26.5 for men and 24.6 for women. In the short-term, there is as a result no simple calculation which establishes definitively whether rates of divorce are going up or down.
25. A small point but an interesting one. Feminist authors sometimes speak of women divorcing in order to reestablish control over their lives. The empirical evidence suggests, on the contrary, that women who divorce typically do so without altering their sense of the extent to which they exercise such control. Drawing on a nationally representative, longitudinal study of 2,864 married, widowed and divorced middle-aged women, Morgan (1988) reports that 'locus of control', as measured by the conventional scale, was typically stable throughout the period of divorce and subsequent readjustment.
26. Hite, p.855 and following. Giddens (1992) says that 'the proportion of women married for more than five years who have had extramarital sexual encounters is today virtually the same as that of men' (p.12). He does not give a reference, but seems to have Hite's inquiries in mind. Later he refers to these as 'marvellously reflexive documents' and draws on them extensively. He says he does this 'without worrying too much about how representative the material is'. The gesture is urbane but also worrying, and for two reasons. The first is that, in Giddens's hands, Hite's material contributes to a sense of looming crisis that may be illusory. The second, that its use fosters the belief, as attractive as it is

seditious, that a scholarly argument about the current state of marriage can be judged by the same criteria as a film script or television advertisement – by its reflexivity, say, or its irony, rather than by its truth.

27. Wellings et al. (1994). The sample was large and carefully selected, and the response rate was by prevailing standards impressive: 71.5% – or 18,876 out of 26,393. The methods used are painstaking. It is nevertheless possible that, especially over matters viewed as embarrassing or shameful, the survey's findings may seriously misrepresent the true state of affairs. With a response rate of 70–75%, a sizeable bias among the respondents in one direction can mask a sizeable bias in the opposite direction in the sample as a whole.

28. Ibid., p.103.

29. Ibid., p.244.

30. Herrnstein and Murray (1994), p.184. Unfortunately, Herrnstein and Murray are themselves a suspect source (see Hudson 1994); nevertheless, their analysis of the National Longitudinal Survey of Youth data deserves serious attention. This survey began in 1979, and embraced 12,686 young men and women, aged between fourteen and twenty-two. Although the sampling was biased to give adequate coverage of minority groups, the data were subsequently normalised to reflect the U.S. population as a whole. The mentally handicapped, on the other hand, were excluded. In 1980, the Department of Defense used the NLSY sample as a test-bed for their newly devised intelligence test, the Armed Forces Qualification Test, which they gave to 94% of the sample. Subsequent interviews have been conducted by the National Opinion Research Council, it being the 1990 wave of interviews on which Herrnstein and Murray draw. In short, their inquiries deal with a nationally representative cross-section of young men and women first seen in the mid-teens to early twenties, and followed as far as their mid-twenties to early thirties. Only the early years of married life are thus covered.

31. Herrnstein and Murray, p.190. The authors separate out whites for purposes of their analysis; but the difficulties experienced by the underclass are those of black and white alike. Indeed, they are accentuated in the case of blacks by the tendency of blacks in America, for whatever reason, to have lower IQ scores than whites.

32. Wellings et al., p.37. In the sample as a whole, first intercourse is most likely to occur within a steady relationship (51% for women, 43% for men); and it is relatively rare for members of either sex to claim that they had been coerced (less than 2% for women, 0.2% of men). Of those who had intercourse for the first time before the age of sixteen, more than half of the women (58%) and nearly a quarter of the men (24%) felt on reflection that they did so too soon. Women were most likely to claim that they had acted as they did because they were 'in love' (39%); men out of 'curiosity' (40%).

33. Ibid., p.48.

5: The Hidden Algebra

1. Barnes (1986). Shrewdly, Giddens (1992) uses this text of Barnes's as

an example. Although we differ from Giddens on many points of principle and substance, he is on fertile ground; and much of this chapter and
the next is shaped in the light of what he says.
2. Barnes, p.13.
3. Ibid., p.36.
4. Ibid., p.24.
5. Ibid., p.25.
6. Ibid., p.115.
7. Ibid., p.50.
8. Rubin (1990).
9. Scruton (1986), p.339. The neglect of sexual jealousy in the psychoanalytic literature is one of that literature's strangest omissions. This is all
the odder in that the phenomena of jealousy reveal so much about the
psychological mechanisms regulating violent emotion. It may well be,
for example, that Graham Kendrick would not have experienced jealous
pangs about Barbara's previous lovers, about Ann's previous husband,
had she had one, or about any lesbian lovers Ann might have had. It
seems that certain categories of sexual rival constitute an existential
threat in ways that other categories do not. More nearly compatible
with orthodox psychoanalytic theorising is the conviction expressed by
Hugh Moreland, one of Anthony Powell's characters, that 'matrimonial
discord vibrates on an axis of envy, rather than jealousy': Powell (1974),
p.45.
10. Lessing (1974).
11. Ibid., p.157.
12. Ibid., p.167.
13. Ibid., p.172.
14. Ibid., p.181.
15. Ibid., p.178.
16. Ibid., p.177.
17. Ibid., p.179.
18. Ibid., p.168.
19. Freud, S., *Collected Papers*, 4, p.213, quoted in Marcuse (1969), p.182.
20. Marcuse (1964), p.56.
21. Ibid., p.77.
22. Henry (1966).
23. Marcus (1966), p.213.
24. Jeremy Bullmore (personal communication). The motives underlying
such discriminations seem at first glance either affiliative or ostentatious.
The indications are, however, that brand-names and logos have a more
primitive lure. It is as if the ordinary acts of life – driving, shopping,
keeping fit – do not really occur unless the actors bear brand-names or
logos as they perform them; that, without those signs and symbols, the
individual's actions lack existential substance.
25. Hirschman (1982), p.21.
26. Ibid., p.16.
27. Marcus, p.180.
28. Hirschman, p.106. Without saying so, Hirschman here draws on first-
hand experience. As a young man, he was a prime mover in the rescue
of Jewish artists and intellectuals from the Nazis, smuggling them across

the frontier between France and Spain. It was a world in which counter-feiting, fraud and deceptions of all kinds were justified by a higher purpose; and in which the immediate risk was that of being arrested, tortured and shot: Carroll (1983). Others who have experienced similar dangers testify to the same sense of freedom: Harry Rée (personal communication).

29. Marcuse (1969) was likewise concerned to reconceive the debate in aesthetic terms. On the other hand, he was content to do so by shuffling the categories of grand theory. The transformation at issue, he assumes, is that of 'sexuality' into 'Eros'; of genitally localised desire into imaginative activity that is eroticised and boundless. He does not attempt to explore or explain the phenomena of the erotic life in terms of those of art, or vice versa; and it is often unclear whether he has in mind what happens in bed, on the picket line, or between the covers of a book.

6: Free for All?

1. Foucault (1981), Derrida (1981), Rorty (1979).
2. If the strengths of the new wisdom are clear to see, so too are its short-comings. The slaughter of Moslem civilians in Bosnia is conventionally viewed as an atrocity and a war crime, but the deconstructive method of reversal and displacement quickly leads to alternative views: that it is a rough-and-ready exercise in freedom fighting, say, or in patriotism. It renders plausible, too, the view that the slaughter is a scare-story got up by Moslems or by the Western media hungry for ratings. The same logic applies to the Holocaust. It is presumably for this reason that Rorty, a warm advocate of the new wisdom, concedes that deconstruction is 'of no political use' (1993, p.248).
3. Giddens (1992). His text has a number of interesting and unexpected features; among them the attention he pays to the beliefs of sexual radicals like Reich and Marcuse. Both envisaged a non-repressive society in which sexual expression is free, in the sense that it is 'increasingly freed from compulsiveness' (p.181). Arguably, on the other hand, desire – like politics and the exercise of the imagination – is a field in which freedom lies in the recognition of necessity.
4. Ibid., p.182.
5. Ibid., p.3. As well as persuasive, one wonders, is this statement actually true? So much depends on the company you keep. The behaviour of those we know accords quite closely with HMSO's divorce statistics and the data in Wellings's (1994) survey. None, male or female, heterosexual or homosexual, seems separated by an emotional abyss from members of the opposite sex.
6. Garber (1993), p.17.
7. Butler (1990), p.xii. Butler argues that the tendency of lesbians to behave either as 'butch' or as 'femme' is a parodic copy of the idea of maleness and femaleness; and that such copies reveal 'the utterly constructed status of the so called heterosexual original. Thus, gay is to straight *not* as copy is to original, but, rather, as copy is to copy' (p.31). But the fact that Y is a parodic copy of X reveals nothing about the

status of X. Nor does the 'original' – that is to say, culturally transmitted norms of heterosexual male and female behaviour, influenced by biology and discovered by each individual in the course of growing up – disappear on the say-so of a polemically inclined individual or group. Were Butler willing to specify the terms on which she would accept behaviour as original rather than copy, this part of her theorising would acquire substance; but she has chosen authorities and texts – Foucault's, for instance – which absolve her from any such responsibility.

8. Welldon (1991) remarks that even the members of her women's groups, highly sophisticated professionals, are at a loss to define the term 'female sexuality', or to separate its meaning from that of femininity, womanhood or motherhood. As Stoller (1979) pointed out, the up-to-date usage of 'sexuality' nonetheless reveals a significant exclusion. It nowadays has only the most tangential bearing on sexual pleasure, and none on the capacity of that pleasure to fuel the imagination.

9. Capote (1988), p.xiii. 'Solipsism' as we use it here is close to the psychoanalytic notion of infantile narcissism (Rycroft 1972).

10. Ibid., p.10.
11. Ibid., p.15.
12. Ibid., p.23.
13. Ibid., p.17.
14. Ibid., p.19.
15. Ibid., p.21.
16. Ibid., p.22.
17. Ibid., p.24.
18. Bowie (1991), p.154.
19. Bowie (1979), p.119.
20. Miller (1993), Lilla (1993).
21. Stoller (1975), p.116; Wellings et al. (1994), p.265.

22. Scruton (1986) makes the case for desire as an interpersonal phenomenon. While finding his argument sympathetic, we feel he overplays his hand. Nothing he says as a philosopher can remove from the purview of the psychologist those up-wellings of desire which are as imperative as they are 'split'.

23. Stoller observes in this context that it is 'the search for (controlled, managed) ambiguity' that characterises sexual excitement and art alike (1975, p.117). We agree with him in seeing familiarity as a pseudo-explanation of failure in sexual relationships, but disagree with his view of the real explanation. 'It is hostility', he says, 'the desire, overt or hidden, to harm another person – that generates and enhances sexual excitement. The absence of hostility leads to sexual indifference and boredom' (Stoller, 1979, p.6). In contrast, we see sexual intimacies running out of meaning, not because the parties to them cannot muster sufficient hostility towards one another, but because they stir Oedipal embers in ways that prove unmanageable.

7: Life and Art

1. Duras (1985), Coward (1990).

2. Another embodiment of driven and systematically maladaptive behaviour in the sexual sphere, also literary, is Anthony Powell's Pamela Flitton. She lays waste most of the men who fall within her grasp (an exception, the necromantic American academic Russell Gwinnett, for whom she commits suicide). The effects were especially damaging, Powell suggests, in those no longer young: 'once pinioned, the middle-aged could be made to writhe almost indefinitely': Spurling (1977), p.64.
3. Duras, p.7.
4. Ibid., p.12.
5. Ibid., p.20.
6. Ibid., p.26.
7. Ibid., p.23.
8. Ibid., p.39. More or less simultaneously with the meeting on the Mekong ferry, but on the other side of the world, the photographer Jacques Henri Lartigue, on the rebound from his wife Bibi's infidelity, was falling in love with the young woman who was to become his mistress, Renée Perle. Like Duras's, Lartigue's art flowed in and out of his life; like Duras, there was within him a sense of alienation or distance: 'my second half, that cold, phlegmatic creature – my self-appointed referee' who 'chuckles in a corner about my performance in real life'. In the autobiographical jottings he attaches to his peerless photographs, first of Bibi and then of Renée, he provides what is, in effect, the reverse angle to Duras's. 'Along the sidewalk of the Rue de la Pompe, I see two women standing in the shadow of a streetlamp. Are they waiting for someone . . . or something? One of the women is tall and slender, the other is tiny. An umbrella next to a pot of flowers. Later, in the Bois, the umbrella is in my car, between the flowers and me . . .' 'Around her I see a halo . . . of magic. At the same time her charm disturbs me. I am afraid it always will. Renée is beautiful; she is tender; she is everything I desire. I live in a dream. But there is one haunting thought: with whom can I expect to talk about love after Renée has gone?' (Lartigue 1978).
9. Duras (1986).
10. Ibid., p.67.
11. Mailer (1980).
12. Duras (1985), p.11.
13. Ibid., p.24.
14. Duras (1986), p.4.
15. Ibid., p.160.
16. The act of writing Duras sees unstably. Sometimes it seems to her that writing possesses a 'basic unseemliness'; that 'if writing isn't all things, all contraries confounded, a quest for vanity and void, it's nothing'. At other times, 'all options' appear open (Duras 1985, p.12).
17. Baron and Shone (1992). Catalogue of the recent Sickert exhibition at the Royal Academy, this acts as an admirable biographical source.
18. Ibid., p.13.
19. White (1977), p.53.
20. Baron and Shone, p.7.
21. *La Hollandaise* is in the Tate Gallery, and is reproduced by Baron and Shone on p.169.

22. Ibid., p.9.
23. Ibid., p.156.
24. Ibid., p.49.
25. Welch (1981), p.25.
26. In important respects, Sickert's personality remained that of the actor he was in his youth. Powell (1983) recalls Sickert's lecture at Oxford in 1923 as a mixture of forceful eccentricity, theatrical flair and sound good sense. 'Tall, grey-haired, crimson in the face, wearing a thick greenish loudly-checked suit, he chatted in a conversational manner, humorous and resonant, while he flourished a cigar. His personality filled the room. Half a century later, I learnt that Sickert (his second wife having died three years before), was still sunk in the deepest depression. No one could have guessed that. On the contrary, he appeared in the best of form, delivering his direct no-nonsense art criticism to an audience of not much more than twenty, most of whom, like myself, probably had little idea what good stuff they were listening to' (p.80).
27. Baron and Shone, p.310.
28. Auerbach (1981), p.7.

8: Parallel Worlds

1. Hobhouse (1988), p.96. The 'object' can perform this existential function, we assume, because rooted in fantasies and recollections of the mother's body. If our arguments about male and female development are sound, it is the female body which is the centrally placed symbol around which, for both sexes, representations of desire revolve. The male body plays a part which is auxiliary and complementary.

   In discussing Duras and Sickert, we have suggested that the existence of art in publicly accessible forms may precede introspection; even be a prior condition of it. Similar-seeming implications stare at one from the history of art; the symbolic exploration of desire in art having reached unrivalled heights of sophistication and vitality at a relatively early date, and in cultures little given to disciplined introspection. In the fourth century BC, Praxiteles translated his model Phryne into the marble statue subsequently known as the Cnidian Venus; a representation of a beautiful woman as a goddess. 'No one questioned the fact', Kenneth Clark says, 'that she was an embodiment of physical desire, and that this mysterious, compulsive force was an element in her sanctity' (1960, p.73). The nature of the psychology of that time is hard to gauge; but some estimate of it can perhaps be derived from the works of Artemidorus, who, some five hundred years later, compiled in his *Oneirocritica* a banal catalogue of dream interpretations conceived as portents or prophecies.
2. Rycroft (1972). Pertinent in this context is Rycroft's observation that the ability to empathise is 'an essential precondition for doing psychoanalytical therapy', and his suggestion that it is an 'example of projective identification'.

   In the late nineteenth century, the founding fathers of experimental psychology made efforts to accommodate empathy to an associationist frame of reference, but failed. Wilhelm Wundt believed that knowledge of another person demanded not only powers of inference, but the ability to re-think one's own personality in the light of the other's. While viewing this process of 'putting oneself into another's Ego' as posing a major problem for psychology, he was unable to resolve it. Others – Theodore Lipps, for instance – treated empathy more nearly behaviourally, as a species of partially internalised imitation (see, e.g., the photograph of bystanders' reactions to a pole vaulter vaulting in Allport 1938, p.530).

Subsequently, experimentally minded psychologists turned their attention elsewhere, but the problem of empathy remains. It is distinct not only from sympathy, but from impersonation of the kind that comes naturally to the character actor.

3. Barthes (1984). The themes of pleasurable surrender, ambiguity and asymmetry are discussed more fully in *The Way Men Think*.

4. Short (1980), p.116. To an extent often unappreciated, the French deconstructive philosophy of the 1970s and 1980s *is* the surrealism of the 1920s and 1930s, translated into an academic context.

5. In making the case for Derrida as a 'sentimental educator', Rorty (1993) implicitly concedes that he is not what those in social science and cultural studies still widely assume him to be: an epistemologist of dazzling rigour and invention. There is a distinction to be drawn between deconstruction as an aid in grasping realities other than our own – a man's if you are a woman, for instance; a heterosexual's if you are homosexual – and deconstruction as a means of establishing what shapes usable knowledge can reasonably be expected to take.

6. Brassaï (1982), p.124.

7. See *The Way Men Think*, p.143.

8. Newton (1989). Newton has expressed puzzlement about why one shot in a long sequence of his own images should prove erotic, while the remainder are merely 'sporty' (Kelly 1979, p.161). The answer, in some cases at least, is plainly formal – a marked tilt from the vertical, for example – not a matter of subject-matter alone.

9. Ricks (1963), pp.136, 137 and 35. Visual images also possess a 'syntax', most obviously when they are paired or grouped; a property that the photographer Ralph Gibson (1983) has made explicit.

10. Progress in this area of theorising has been slower than it otherwise might have been because psychologists have tended either to treat convergent and divergent reasoning as discrete facets of human intelligence (Guilford 1950), or to balance one against the other in order to identify psychological types (Getzels and Jackson 1962; Hudson 1966).

11. Such modelling envisages an *array*, which is made up of *elements*, each of which possesses a variety of *features*. A poem, let us say, has four elements: the unicorn, the moon, the maiden, the mirror. If the unicorn and the moon are likened in terms of their purity, significant differences between them are thrown automatically into relief: that one is alive, the other inanimate, and so on. Features excluded from the first perception of similarity-in-difference become the basis for further such perceptions: the unicorn and the maiden are both alive; the moon and mirror are

both inanimate; the unicorn and the mirror are both in their own ways sources of illusion; and so on. Any such an array, it follows, can be read in a rich (although not infinitely rich) variety of ways. It is from these alternative readings that there emerges a sense both of the array's implicit themes, and of the patterns of consonance and dissonance between them.

12. Although elements of an individual's personality or a close relationship are not given in the way that those of a poem or photograph are, standard psychological techniques like repertory grid analysis (Kelly 1955) exist to elicit certain of them.

13. Broadly, such thinking is 'hermeneutic'. Drawn from German biblical scholarship, the term originally referred both to the search for the best reading of obscure or corrupted texts, and to the updating of the Christian message of those texts in order to render them intelligible to subsequent generations. Late in the nineteenth century, the term was imported from theology to philosophy by Wilhelm Dilthey, and was used in characterising what is distinctive about the human (as opposed to the biological or physical) sciences; the sciences, that is to say, essentially concerned with issues of meaning or *Verstehen*.

Some philosophers – Charles Taylor (1971), for instance – have since sought to justify a clear boundary of principle separating the human from the biological or physical; but have done so at the cost of muddle and inaccuracy. What, for example, is to be said about techniques like the semantic differential (Osgood, Suci and Tannenbaum 1957) or the repertory grid, which deal in meanings but generate numerical data which are handled impersonally?

Still unresolved is the question of whether the human sciences are *about* meaning, but are in other respects as factual as, say, biology; or, like literary criticism and speculative philosophy, they *consist of* meanings (Skinner 1985). Granted such uncertainty, it is only to be expected that the term 'hermeneutic' should now be used somewhat indiscriminately – as, for instance, in justifying the carefree approach to factual evidence of the Hite Reports (Hite 1988, p.770).

9: Issues of Principle: a Conjecture

1. Collingwood (1963), p.288.
2. Rorty (1993), Lyotard (1993).
3. Bateson (1979), p.69.
4. The various roles that principles can play within a close relationship remain to be established. A value like equality, we are going to claim, is a discovery that some individuals make in the context of an erotic intimacy. Clearly, however, it can also act as a self-sustaining myth which a couple evolve collusively, in a spirit of systematic self-deception.

There exists an important therapeutic tradition which treats the close relationship as a psychological entity in its own right (Dicks 1967). Such a relationship is seen as constituting a psychic system which embodies preoccupations, defences and fantasies which are shared, and which can be analysed as though they were those of a single person. The bias of our own argument is more individualistic. We assume that the close relationship is a 'container' within which the needs and fantasies of the two parties are often discrepant, and within which what is shared (and shareable) is always in question.

5. White (1977), p.53.
6. While in Dieppe in the early 1920s, Sickert produced a series of images of players in the Casino. Elsewhere, more or less simultaneously, Vuillard was drawing and painting groups playing bridge (Baron and Shone 1992, p.268). Even the most fastidious expert, if faced with such works blind – shorn, that is to say, of their signatures and provenances – would have difficulty in ascribing these works to one artist or the other.
7. 'A woman's head has just produced in me a certain emotion,' Vuillard's journal for 1890 records, 'I must make use of this emotion alone and I must not try to remember the nose or the ear, they're of no importance' (Thomson 1991, p.10). Predictably perhaps but also paradoxically, it was this philosophy not Sickert's which was to lead in the end to the stronger sense of objectivity and of place. Sickert's, in contrast, led to forms of image-making which were both revolutionary and quirky.
8. At this point, needless to say, our argument becomes sharply reflexive. Polemicists like Millett, social scientists like Mead and Giddens, philosophers like Foucault, Derrida and Rorty, do not stand outside what they profess, we assume; they profess as they do in order to deny what they fear and legitimate what they desire. We are in no way exempt. We write to resist what we find menacing, and to protect the visions of felicity on which our equilibria depend. The question then arises of whether there exist means of escape from these cycles of self-defence and self-legitimation. In the belief that there do, we point both to the kinds of knowledge that intimacy and art generate, and to those forms of academic discipline which enable otherness to be recognised, not as we might wish it to be, but as it is.
9. Hayward (1955), p.3.
10. Beeching (1952). Until recently, the overwhelming tendency in enlightened circles has been to treat chastity as a joke. An exception is Scruton (1986). Having done battle for more than three hundred pages with biological views of desire and with the Platonic distinction between sexual desire and erotic love, he proposes chastity as the value which allows the individual – like Bernini's 'St. Teresa' – to embody desire without needing automatically to express it physically; a distinction close to that drawn by Marcuse (1964, 1969) and Brown (1959, 1966) between genitally localised expressions of desire and the more diffusely erotic. Almost as an afterthought, Scruton defends 'bourgeois' marriage against Foucault; but offers nothing to comfort or persuade those seriously in doubt about that institution's present or future well-being.

In part at least, chastity and its implications have been ignored for commercial reasons. As Cline (1993) says, sex sells. 'The most insidious workings of the genital myth', she points out, 'operate within and as an integral part of a culture where the seven billion dollar pornography industry (now the largest media category) trades innocently as erotica' (p.6). This culture actively promotes the belief that while 'in reality individual sexual acts may be felt to be uncomfortable or unspeakable', all sexual acts are in principle physically beneficial, morally sound, normal.

11. The meanings the OED gives for 'chaste' are:

Pure from unlawful sexual intercourse; continent, virtuous;

Celibate, single (1596);

Morally pure, innocent (1535);

Decent; free from indecency or offensiveness (1621);

Chastened; restrained from all excess (1774).

Here we move beyond the dictionary definition, taking 'chastity' to mean a principled commitment which treats exclusive relationships of mutual love and trust as the only form of relationship appropriate to the expression of sexual desire. It abutts, accordingly, the conventional notions of 'respectability' and 'self-respect'.

12. Wilson (1983), p.44. Wilson is especially helpful in that he brings alive the doctrinal context of Milton's life and work.
13. Ibid., p.44.
14. Ibid., p.39.
15. Ibid., p.31.
16. Ibid., p.176.
17. Ibid., p.34.
18. Broadbent (1960), p.44.
19. Wilson, p.52. As an adolescent, Cardinal Newman came to the conclusion that there were 'two and only two supreme and luminously self-evident beings, myself and my Creator' (ibid., p.175). Milton, Wilson remarks, could as well have said the same.
20. Broadbent, p.34.
21. Marcus (1966), p.152. The author of *My Secret Life* was by no means alone. Hyam (1990) quotes the Reverend Charles Kingsley, author of *The Water Babies* and *Hereward the Wake*, as writing to his wife in 1843 about his vision of heaven as allowing uninterrupted sexual pleasure. The 'thrilling writhings' that they enjoy in one another's arms are, he suggests, 'but dim shadows of a union which shall be perfect' (p.58).
22. Marcus, p.159.
23. Ibid., p.144.
24. Ibid., p.139.
25. Ibid., p.144.
26. Ibid., p.146.
27. Ibid., p.148.

References

Abraham, R. H. and Shaw, C. D., *Dynamics – The Geometry of Behavior*, Aerial Press, 1988.

Allport, G. W., *Personality*, Constable, 1938.

Auerbach, F., Foreword, in *Late Sickert*, Arts Council of Great Britain, 1981.

Bailey, H., *Vera Brittain*, Penguin, 1987.

Barham, D., *Ms London*, p.3, 14 November 1994.

Barnes, J., *Before She Met Me*, Picador, 1986.

Baron, W. and Shone, R. (eds), *Sickert Paintings*, Yale University Press, 1992.

Barthes, R., *Camera Lucida*, Fontana, 1984.

Bateson, G., *Steps to an Ecology of Mind*, Ballantine Books, 1972.

Bateson, G., *Mind and Nature*, Wildwood House, 1979.

Becker, J., *Hitler's Children*, Pickwick Books, 1989.

Beeching, H. C. (ed.), *The Poetical Works of John Milton*, Oxford University Press, 1952.

Bowie, M., Jacques Lacan, in *Structuralism and Since*, ed. J. Sturrock, Oxford University Press, 1979.

Bowie, M., *Lacan*, Fontana, 1991.

Bowlby, J., *A Secure Base*, Basic Books, 1988.

Brassai, *The Artists of My Life*, Thames and Hudson, 1982.

Breen, D., General introduction, in *The Gender Conundrum*, ed. D. Breen, Routledge, 1993.

Broadbent, J. B., *Some Graver Subject*, Chatto and Windus, 1960.

Brockman, J. (ed.), *About Bateson*, Wildwood House, 1978.

Brown, N. O., *Life Against Death*, Wesleyan University Press, 1959.

Brown, N. O., *Love's Body*, Random House, 1966.

Butler, J., *Gender Trouble*, Routledge, 1990.

Capote, T., *Answered Prayers*, Abacus, 1988.

Carroll, D., Escape from Vichy, *American Heritage*, June/July 1983.

Chodorow, N. J., *The Reproduction of Mothering*, University of California Press, 1978.
Clark, K., *The Nude*, Penguin, 1960.
Cline, S., *Women, Celibacy and Passion*, André Deutsch, 1993.
Collingwood, R. G., *The Principles of Art*, Oxford University Press, 1963.
Coward, D., Marguerite Duras, in *Beyond the Nouveau Roman*, ed. M. Tilby, Berg, 1990.
Critchlow, K., *Order in Space*, Thames and Hudson, 1969.

Derrida, J., *Positions*, Athlone, 1981.
Dicks, H. *Marital Tensions*, Routledge & Kegan Paul, 1967.
Duras, M., *The Lover*, Collins, 1985.
Duras, M., *La Douleur*, Collins, 1986.

Eichenbaum, L. and Orbach, S., *What Do Women Want?*, Harper Collins, 1994.
Engels, F., *The Origin of the Family*, Lawrence and Wishart, 1942.

Festy, P., *Divorce, Judicial Separation and Remarriage*, Council of Europe Population Studies 17, 1985.
Fortune, R., Arapesh warfare, *American Anthropologist*, 41, 1, 1939.
Foucault, M., *The History of Sexuality*, Penguin, 1981.
Freeman, D., *Margaret Mead and Samoa: the Making and Unmaking of an Anthropological Myth*, Harvard University Press, 1983.
Freeman, D., There's tricks i' th' world, *Visual Anthropology Review*, 7, 103, 1991.
Freud, S., *The Aetiology of Hysteria*, 1896, Standard Edition, 3, ed. J. Strachey, Hogarth, 1957–74.
Freud, S., *My Views on the Part Played by Sexuality in the Aetiology of the Neuroses*, 1905, Standard Edition, 7, ed. J. Strachey, Hogarth, 1957–74.
Freud, S., *Autobiographical Study*, 1925, Standard Edition, 20, ed. J. Strachey, Hogarth, 1957–74.

Garber, M., *Vested Interests*, Penguin, 1993.
Getzels, J. W. and Jackson, P. W., *Creativity and Intelligence*, Wiley, 1962.
Gibson, R., *Syntax*, Lustrum, 1983.
Giddens, A., *The Transformation of Intimacy*, Polity, 1992.
Gilligan, C., *In a Different Voice*, Harvard University Press, 1982.

Greenson, R. R., Dis-identifying from mother: its special importance for the boy, *International Journal of Psycho-Analysis*, 49, 370, 1968.
Grove, V., Somerville girls, *Life and Times*, 7 February 1992.
Guilford, J. P., Creativity, *American Psychologist*, 5, 444, 1950.

Hayward, J. (ed.), *John Donne, Complete Poetry and Selected Prose*, Nonesuch, 1955.
Henry, J., *Culture Against Man*, Tavistock, 1966.
Herrnstein, R. J., and Murray, C., *The Bell Curve*, Free Press, 1994.
Hirschman, A. O., *Shifting Involvements*, Martin Robertson, 1982.
Hite, S., *Women and Love*, Viking, 1988.
Hobhouse, J., *The Bride Stripped Bare*, Cape, 1988.
Hodgkin, D., in *A Passion for Science*, ed. L. Wolpert and A. Richards, Oxford University Press, 1988.
Hopkins, J., The probable role of trauma in a case of foot and shoe fetishism, *International Review of Psychoanalysis*, 11, 79, 1984.
Howard, J., *Margaret Mead*, Harvill, 1984.
Hudson, L., *Contrary Imaginations*, Methuen, 1966.
Hudson, L., *Human Beings*, Cape, 1975.
Hudson, L., The wretched connection, *Times Literary Supplement*, 2 December 1994.
Hudson, L., and Jacot, B., *The Way Men Think*, Yale University Press, 1991.
Hyam, R., *Empire and Sexuality*, Manchester University Press, 1990.

Israels, H. and Schatzman, M., The seduction theory, *History of Psychiatry*, 4, 23, 1993.

Jack, D. C., *Silencing the Self*, Harvard University Press, 1991.
Johnson-Laird, P. N. and Oatley, K., The language of emotions: an analysis of a semantic field, *Cognition and Emotion*, 3, 81, 1989.
Junor, P., *Margaret Thatcher*, Sidgwick and Jackson, 1983.

Keller, E. F., *Reflections on Gender and Science*, Yale University Press, 1985.
Kelly, G. A., *The Psychology of Personal Constructs*, Norton, 1955.
Kelly, J., *Nude: Theory*, Lustrum, 1979.
Koestler, A., *The Sleepwalkers*, Hutchinson, 1959.
Kuhn, T. S., *The Structure of Scientific Revolutions*, Chicago University Press, 1962.
Kuper, A., Coming of age in anthropology?, *Nature*, 338, 453, 1989.

Lartigue, J. H., *Diary of a Century*, Penguin, 1978.

Leishman, J. B., and Spender, S., *Duino Elegies*, Hogarth, 1952.

Lessing, D., *The Temptation of Jack Orkney and Other Stories*, Bantam, 1974.

Lilla, M., A taste for pain, *Times Literary Supplement*, 26 March 1993.

Lipset, D., Gregory Bateson: Early biography, in *About Bateson*, ed. J. Brockman, Wildwood House, 1978.

Lyotard, J.-F., The other's rights, in *On Human Rights*, ed., S. Shute and S. Hurley, Basic Books, 1993.

MacDonald, E., *Shoot the Women First*, Fourth Estate, 1991.

Mailer, N., *The Executioner's Song*, Arrow, 1980.

Marcus, S., *The Other Victorians*, Weidenfeld & Nicolson, 1966.

Marcuse, H., *One-Dimensional Man*, Routledge & Kegan Paul, 1964.

Marcuse, H., *Eros and Civilization*, Sphere, 1969.

Marriage and Divorce Statistics, 1837–1983, HMSO, 1990.

Marriage and Divorce Statistics, 1991, HMSO, 1993.

Mead, M., *Sex and Temperament*, Morrow, 1935.

Mead, M., *Coming of Age in Samoa*, Penguin, 1969.

Miller, J., *The Passion of Michel Foucault*, Simon & Schuster, 1993.

Millett, K., *Sexual Politics*, Doubleday, 1970.

Millett, K., *The Loony Bin Trip*, Virago, 1991.

Morgan, L. A., Locus of control and marital termination, *Journal of Divorce*, 11, 35, 1988.

Morgan, R., *The Demon Lover*, Methuen, 1989.

Newton, H., *Helmut Newton*, Thames and Hudson, 1989.

Osgood, C. E., Suci, G. J. and Tannenbaum, P. H., *The Measurement of Meaning*, Illinois University Press, 1957.

Place, U. T., The role of the ethnomethodological experiment in the empirical investigation of social norms and its application to conceptual analysis, *Philosophy of the Social Sciences*, 22(4), 461, 1992.

Post, J. M. and Robins, R. S., *When Illness Strikes the Leader*, Yale University Press, 1993.

Powell, A., *Temporary Kings*, Fontana, 1974.

Powell, A., *To Keep the Ball Rolling*, Penguin, 1983.

Radloff, L. S., Risk factors for depression, in *The Mental Health of Women*, ed. M. Guttentag, S. Salasin and D. Belle, Academic Press, 1980.

Redfearn, J. W. T., When are things persons and persons things?, *Journal of Analytical Psychology*, 27, 215, 1982.

Ricks, C., *Milton's Grand Style*, Oxford University Press, 1963.

Roazen, P., *Brother Animal*, Allen Lane, 1970.

Roe, A., A psychological study of eminent psychologists and anthropologists and a comparison with biological and physical scientists, *Psychological Monographs*, 67, no. 352, 1953.

Rorty, R., *Philosophy and the Mirror of Nature*, Princeton University Press, 1979.

Rorty, R., Human rights, rationality, and sentimentality, in *On Human Rights*, ed., S. Shute and S. Hurley, Basic Books, 1993.

Rubin, L., *Erotic Wars*, Farrar, Straus and Giroux, 1990.

Rycroft, C., *A Critical Dictionary of Psychoanalysis*, Penguin, 1972.

Rycroft, C., *Psychoanalysis and Beyond*, Chatto and Windus, 1985.

Schatzman, M., Freud: who seduced whom?, *New Scientist*, 34, 21 March 1992.

Scruton, R., *Sexual Desire*, Weidenfeld and Nicolson, 1986.

Short, R., *Dada and Surrealism*, Octopus, 1980.

Skinner, Q. (ed.), *The Return of Grand Theory in the Human Sciences*, Cambridge University Press, 1985.

Sorensen, R. A., *Thought Experiments*, Oxford University Press, 1992.

Spurling, H., *Handbook to Anthony Powell's Music of Time*, Heinemann, 1977.

Stern, D., *The Interpersonal World of the Infant*, Basic Books, 1985.

Stoller, R. J., Symbiosis anxiety and the development of masculinity, *Archives of General Psychiatry*, 30, 164, 1974.

Stoller, R. J., *Perversion*, Pantheon, 1975.

Stoller, R. J., *Sexual Excitement*, Pantheon, 1979.

Storr, A., *Solitude*, Collins, 1988.

Sulloway, F., *Freud, Biologist of the Mind*, Burnett, 1979.

Taylor, C., Interpretation and the sciences of man, *Review of Metaphysics*, 25, 3, 1971.

Thomson, B., *Vuillard*, South Bank Centre, 1991.

Tillich, H., *From Time to Time*, Stein and Day, 1974.

Trevarthen, C. and Logotheti, K., Child and culture, in *Cognition and Social Worlds*, ed. A. Gellaty, D. Rogers and J. A. Sloboda, Oxford University Press, 1989.

Weissman, M. M., Gender and depression, in *Women and Depression*, ed. R. Formanek and A. Gurian, Springer, 1987.

Welch, D., Sickert at St. Peter's, in *Late Sickert*, Arts Council of Great Britain, 1981.

Welldon, E. V., Psychology and psychopathology in women, *British Journal of Psychiatry*, 158, 85, 1991.

Wellings, K., Field, J., Johnson, A. M. and Wadsworth, J., *Sexual Behaviour in Britain*, Penguin, 1994.

White, G., in *Sickert*, Arts Council of Great Britain, 1977.

Wilson, A. N., *The Life of John Milton*, Oxford University Press, 1983.

Young, H., *One of Us*, Macmillan, 1989.

Young-Bruehl, E., *Anna Freud*, Macmillan, 1989.

Zilbach, J. J., Female Adolescence, in *Female Adolescent Development*, ed. M. Sugar, Brunner/Mazel, 1993.

Index of Names